MY INVISIBLE FRIENDS

*An inspirational true story
of a quirky soul's journey*

ISBN: 979-8-218-40791-9

Book Cover Artwork:
Title "Beyond". Watercolor painting by
Terrie Sue Townsend (color edited from original).
Terrie Sue is a contemporary, expressionistic, mix-media
artist residing in Bayfield, Wisconsin.

Printed in the United States of America

MY INVISIBLE FRIENDS

An inspirational true story of a quirky soul's journey

Marisalena Manchego

For all the misfits, the lost ones, the harried ones, the brave-faced ones, for all parents who always do the best they can in every given situation with the tools they have at the time, for all children who are always born beautiful and beloved, and to their sweet spirits that always endure; this is for you. May you rediscover your truth, your light, your cherished preciousness and your laughter.

ACKNOWLEDGMENTS

What is an acknowledgement but another way of saying thank you and of all the expressions we can make in life, gratitude is foremost the most powerful and precious of them all.

So from my heart, I offer deep thanks to many sundry beings, but I shall speak of only a few here. In the practical, earthly sense, Rafael Manchego, my friend through thick and thin, in this lifetime and others, your patience, loyalty, love and wise words temper and ground me. Terrie Sue Townsend, my dear friend who reminded me of whimsey and the beauty of wordsmithing, Joanne DeMichele who set me on the structured real-time path of writing and editing, John LeMay, the indelible author extraordinaire and tech savvy formatting friend after my own heart, the other author friends whose works I also recommend reading and who generously shared their wisdom when I asked, Sandra Hayes, Michelle Morrison, MC Lorbiecke, Stacy Tatum, and Ted Schooley. My Brother from another Mother, Craig Farkas, who both helps me stay sane and drives me crazy, but always with lots of laughter and love, my beloved Dance Sisters of my heart and my family, blood and otherwise, that loves me, no matter what; to all of you I am eternally grateful.

To my ancestors, guides, helpers, angels, wisdom holders and dimensional buddies, it's been a slice, as a Portuguese friend of mine used to say, and I look forward to eating more pie of our shared exploits.

To you, My Dear Readers, I am grateful you are here and I wish you Big Fat Beautiful Blessings of Renewal, Hope and Peace!

My heart overflowing with love at the gift of her, I said,
"I wish I could be a dragon!"
She lowered her huge head to me and gently surrounded
me with her warm, moist, brimstone breath saying,
"You were."
~encounter in a camper~

CONTENTS

INTRODUCTION

The summer of 2021, I began having a vague idea periodically surface that I needed to write something; something that was important. Not just my occasional dream interpretation, or my sometimes very good poetry or the "some day I'm going to write that novel" lament. I felt I might be getting an angelic nudge or a guide-provoked elbow in the ribs telling me I really needed to share my (pretty weird, sometimes fascinating) story about the things that have happened in my life, because other people might need to hear it as a help or inspiration in their own lives.

This came part and parcel with my inner knowing that it was time to finally be myself. Fully. It was time to not withhold my spiritual experiences from people because of what they might think, truly more of what my friends, family, peers, clients and students might think. Yes, I talk to trees and understand what they say back. I can hear a bird communicate intentions and meanings if I want. I can see and/or feel a guide, sprite, earth diva, angel, ancestor, sometimes a star-partner, and as I evolve, my abilities evolve. This is part of who I am and I am not keeping me a secret any longer.

Things were not always like this and I was not always like that. But I, like so very many people, had experiences as a toddler and child that were wondrous and I thought, normal, for everyone. Like many people, when I tried to share what I saw, heard or felt, I was corrected by a well-meaning adult enough times that I pushed my special times down into the depths of my psyche and they were soon buried beneath the bigness of life.

This book is absolutely not about me being some amazingly gifted spiritual guru, but about "owning" my fuller self and being ok with that. This book is also not about my desire for anyone who reads it to devote their lives to some concept of a spiritual practice. *My Invisible Friends* is just about me sharing my self, in a vulnerable, tender and possibly kind of funny way, in hopes the reader will connect with it and remember their own fuller self with love and acceptance. I want to normalize talking about Spirituality.

At the very least, this is certainly an entertaining read.

In spring of 2022, I started participating in an occasional free writing "master class" offered by two different authors and another couple classes offered by two different publishing companies. I learned some very valuable do's and don'ts of writing. Meanwhile, the subject matter of my book began solidifying like a misty apparition finally making itself visible.

Shoot forward to late July. I was sitting in my back yard, bare feet on the ground, listening to the water fountain in the shade of the pecan tree, avoiding the already intense New Mexico summer sun. I was doing my daily tapping points with my affirmations, my morning "prayers" as it were. This "book thing" was hanging around in the back of my brain since those classes, and all of a sudden the words "My Invisible Friends" placed themselves in my frontal cortex. "YES!! That's it!!!" said my frontal cortex.

I began carving time out and started writing my story. When I got to areas of reveal that caused some concern or discomfort, I sometimes hesitated, sent my trusty "antenna" out (read on, it will become clearer), and would hear, "It's important." Trusting the input, I would forge on. Lot's of life happened, including a little Covid and oh, that time I broke my back. A funny thing happened on the way to the bedroom.

But what also happened is that I kept having more memory come up about some things; my sister's torture, for instance. I had much of my own emotion I had to recognize, facilitate and take time for throughout the book. What a wonderful clearing process this has been for me and I am eternally grateful to my family and friends, ever-lovin' guides, angels, ancestors, and the "rest of yas" as my New Yorker friend says.

A few points of interest:

1) I am no expert of anything. Just my life, kinda sorta.

2) I use terms to suit my own needs. For instance: "astral/etheric" bodies are interchangeable to best interpret my feeling at the event-time. Deepest Soul Self also fits my encompassing best sense of our bodies being fully immersed and held within our larger soul, being connected to full Source-God-Universe. Invisible Friends and Spirit Partners are ultimately the same thing.

3) I do not attempt to diagnose or recommend treatment of any kind. If a therapy or activity I practiced or underwent appeals to you in the larger sense of your own physical-mental-emotional-spiritual well-being, I suggest you talk to your health care or other professional for valuable support and/or input if you have any self-doubts.

4) You don't have to believe anything I say. Take what works for you and just have fun with it!

5) I have changed the name of everyone in the book, except for me, of course, and my beloved junior high school and high school musical director. He saved my life and even though he isn't embodied anymore, I am proud to put his name in front of anyone that reads this.

I shall close now. It is time to sit outside in the lovely New Mexico spring sunshine, kick my shoes off to feel Mama Earth under my feet for 10 minutes or so, breathe and be grateful!

CHAPTER 1
When I Flew

I could fly by the time I could walk, or nearly so.

We moved to London, Kentucky, in early winter of 1958. It's beautiful little knobs of hills are a part of the Appalachian Mountain Chain, which begins in Newfoundland, and in the United States, Maine, and ends in central Georgia and Northern Alabama. London felt like home to my cells and heart being as I was born in the Great Smokey Mountains, a hop and a skip south into Tennessee. I was 18 months old when we moved there and we left a year later. These events happened during that year.

I have my first embodied memories there; my Sister and I hanging doll blankets across the old, open end table making the perfect curtain for our puppet show stage, and waiting impatiently in our front yard at the side of the road in the afternoon of a weekday for Elise's school bus to pull up, releasing my best friend back to me so my real life could begin again. One time she brought me a present from school, a shiny, red rubber coin purse that would open by squeezing it. It had a smell unlike any I'd smelled before or since. I kept it for years.

I remember playing with the big whistle on a heavy chain that Mom would blow to call Elise home from her friend's house across the road (that I was not allowed to cross of course, being just a toddler), and my favorite game of all, rolling down the hill in back of our house, stopping just short of the creek, breathless, excited and slightly battered. I recall my tiny body catching air. I LOVED it!

Maybe that is what gave me the idea to try my flying skills in our basement, away from my Mother's overseeing eyes. I had played in the basement before with Sister, or I played as Mom did laundry and ironed Dad's shirts, sprinkling fine droplets of water from a coke bottle with a nozzle made just for that purpose. It was always a one-at-a-time step venture for my chubby little legs to climb up and down, but I confidently did so, with one hand on a rail above me, or sometimes holding Mom's hand.

Now, as I try to bring to mind how many steps the stairs had, I am not positive. I didn't have words for counting then, but I know the house was built on a hill, the basement ceiling was high above my tall Mother's head, and the stairs were wooden with wooden handrails on each side. As I recollect the particulars of this event for this book, I question how I could touch both handrails at the same time. My Mother was 5'11", Pop was 6'2" and I know my fingertips could touch both handrails before liftoff.

One day when Dad was at work, Sister was at school and Mom was busy doing things that housewives did during those days, I tiptoed to the basement door, quietly opened it, stepped in and silently closed it behind me. I instinctively knew I did not want my Mother involved in this adventure.

I made my way down to the bottom of the stairs and stood on the first step. I jumped off and landed safely. I then climbed to the next step and jumped again, landing safely. I climbed my way up to the third step, confident and happy how my experiment was going. I looked at the distance to the basement floor, and this is when I had the instinctive idea to use the handrails (not that I REALIZED that was their name) to give me more lift to make it all the way to the floor. I put my tiny hands on the wood, fingertips touching, jumped, went up higher as I'd expected, and softly landed.

I was methodical, never expecting failure, only success. I repeated, always knowing I would lift off and land easily on the basement floor. There was no thought of safety or doubt.

I distinctly remember standing on the next to the highest step, fingertips primed, legs slightly bent in liftoff mode, when the door jerked open and my Mother loudly exclaimed "WHAT ARE YOU DOING?" Her fear and chastisement about hurting myself permeated me as she took my hand, lifted me up onto safe ground, closed the basement door and said "Never again, do you hear me!"

I don't know if it was days or weeks that went by before I snuck into the basement alone to see if I could fly again. I stood on the bottom step feeling slightly fearful, and jumped. There was no lightness of feeling, a heavy landing. I climbed up to the next step, fully felt what was now my fear, and changed my mind. I was afraid to fly. I would hurt myself.

I had a boyfriend several years ago that had St. Vitas' Dance as a young child; a horrible disease that took nearly a year from which to recover. He spent many months in a bunkbed, with a heavy blankct hanging around the perimeter of his bed to keep the light from paining his eyes, unable to voluntarily move his body. His mother tended to him daily, washing, cleaning and feeding him. One evening, his family gathered as usual around the dinner table and he was desperate to be there with them. All of a sudden, he was! He was SO excited, he loudly exclaimed to his parents, his siblings, over and over again to look at him, see him and what he could do! No one saw or heard him. That was the day he found a new freedom.

That boy learned amazing skills and grew into an unbelievably gifted man. That is his story to tell, but I am sharing this with you because he also flew as a child. I do not know if it was before or after his illness. He shared with me that he was standing one day at the foot of the biggest, most beautiful tree on their farm, and he very much wanted to be able to climb it to the top. It was impossible as the branches were so high up. He recollects his yearning, and then moving up into the branches. He was thrilled! He didn't wonder why or how it happened. He wondered if he could do it again, so he came down, gently touched and went back up. I am certain there were no adults around or anyone else to tell him he couldn't do it. He did it a couple more times that day, and then again not too long after. As I said, the rest is his story to tell.

How many times have we seen babies staring diligently at "nothing"? Or see our dogs or cats staring at an area of the room or better yet, watched them see something move about the room that was not a fly or other bug?

When our children are two, three and four years old we start "teaching" them colors. These are the precious years when they are still seeing things we are not seeing, when what some call "the veil" between worlds is still sometimes quite transparent. A child very well may know they are seeing a bright blue cloud or as we know it, aura, around Grandpa which is much brighter than that sweater he is wearing. Of course the child sees the brilliant blue instead of the green wool.

If a child gets told enough times by a well-intentioned adult that they are wrong, no, that is the wrong word for that color, or they didn't see Grandma in the corner because she's with God now and not here, or to not climb that tree because they will hurt themselves, we do them a disservice. As children, we adults had been told many times that our perceptions or choices were wrong, and most times our "vision" or "inner knowing" shut down to protect ourselves and/or to please our loved ones. Is it possible or even probable that, as adults, it is our own fear that we project or actually send into our children that then causes them to loose their inner sense of balance or knowing and they then fall?

Our Deepest Soul Selves know what is right and true, that we are brilliant and beloved Souls temporarily inhabiting these amazing physical bodies. Our Deepest Soul Selves "remember" our true natures and that we have a plethora of loving angels, ancestors, guides, earth energies and more that support us, help us, and endeavor to assist us in gaining back our memory of what is possible for us. Our Deepest Soul Selves know what science has been studying in the last 35 years, Psychoneuroimmunology, which is the effect on our bio-systems by our thought patterns that create well-being or the opposite of the same.

This is not new knowledge or information. There is much in our written and oral history of ancient mystery schools around the world that knew Body, Mind and Spirit is truly one. There is a deeper knowing available to us that we were born with and maybe, just maybe you picked up this book to know that you are not alone in wondering if there is more.

I am sharing my story with you because if I can help anyone in learning to trust themselves again, their deepest felt sense, their highest wisdom, their intuition, to create an ease and trust in life, a knowing of peace and that all is well within the apparent turmoil in life, than I am deeply grateful.

CHAPTER TWO
My Secret Garden

At two and a half years old, we moved to Eastern Ohio, east of Zanesville, at the top of a hill off a country lane. We were now at a western foot of the Appalachian Mountain Chain. I wish I could show you pictures of this fantasy world of nature in which I was blessed to grow up. Huge bushes of pink and red wild roses, rambling honeysuckle, purple and white lilac bushes bigger than our car, yellow fragrant forsythia and a gigantic white snowball bush that spanned the width of the kitchen outside the windows, were a constant from late spring to early fall. Wildflowers, including wild Irises, grew everywhere.

Huge trees dotted our hillsides and I became friends with most of them. Tall, stately pines, oak, maple, buckeye, chestnut, beech, crabapple, redbud, dogwood, elm and more, with my beloved favorite, a towering, expansive weeping willow with a glorious canopy to shelter me. I had lots of delightful, gratifying playtime and scabs from these trees.

In the summer, after doing our chores, my Sister and I would roam the hillside, barefoot usually, picking blackberries or raspberries and eating them as fast as we could pluck them off the thorny branches. Sometimes, we brought some home to Mom who'd make cobbler with them for supper's dessert. When people ask me where I grew up, I reply "outside."

This is where my true education of the way of the world began and my Sister was my Great Teacher. Nearly every day until winter, we would spend time chin in hand, laying on the ground, watching and interacting with bugs, spiders, worms, ladybugs, snakes and whatever creatures lived on that level. Once I showed my Grandpa my newly found "worms" when, in fact, I had a nest of baby garter snakes in my tiny hands. I learned early on how to tell the upcoming weather by the wooly worms. I began to know these ground living creatures as individuals and friends, and their families, my friends. Elise told me stories about the faeries and we would find the perfect houses where they lived; under this toadstool or in those flowers. We would follow the numerous butterflies, hummingbirds and at nighttime, lightening bugs, knowing the faeries sometimes caught rides on these little flying wonders. Sometimes we caught glimpses of them on their backs as we became trusted friends of these magical creatures.

It became a given, in growing up, that elves, sprites, gnomes and faeries exist and are always to be found if one looks hard enough. How much of this knowing was pure imagination, inspiration or possibly the truth? In Latin, Truth's meaning; Imaginari, Inspiratio/Soul, Spiritus/ Breath, Wind, Truth/Fides/Faith, Trust, Belief. To this day, I still share with young ones the excitement and mystery of where they may find our woods', deserts' and plains' small magical creatures, because magic does, indeed, exist.

As I grew older I encouraged my particular "veil" of awareness to grow more transparent which allowed me to see and interact with the plant divas and spirits. I learned that as young children, we see what we can interpret, as a Tinkerbell-like fairy was provided by my brain to my eyes because I understood that. As an adult, I see plant spirit sometimes as white/gold glowing orbs, or have a felt sense of presence when I am near a tree or plant that wishes to communicate. Sometimes I will see a movement of light out of the corner of my eye and hear or "feel" words or intentions of feelings.

But I am getting ahead of my story. This is not about you immediately going out to become the "Plant Whisperer". This is about knowing that nature is our biggest tutor when it comes to allowing our Deepest Soul Selves to gently emerge, dusting themselves off from where they've been hiding, hoping to be treated kindly like we wanted to be treated when we were little, before being shut down.

So consider, if you are in a city surrounded by buildings, sit for a little while with a beautiful plant. Breathe, admire, feel gratitude, repeat. Wherever you are with either a lot or a wee bit of nature, be still, for a bit, breathe, admire, feel gratitude, repeat. Do this regularly. Then begin to allow a bird, the birds, an insect, a moth or spider, to be noticed by you. Be still, breathe, admire, feel gratitude, repeat. Notice if you get an intuition or memory. There may be some wisdom here for you. Be still, breathe, admire, feel gratitude...

CHAPTER 3
My Invisible World

Nowadays, if one wants to travel from Zanesville, Ohio to Toledo, one takes I70 West to Columbus and then north on State 23 eventually arriving in Toledo. When I first lived in the little house atop the hill seven miles east of Zanesville, the valley spread below us, creating an idyllic country scene and the single laned road far below ran from Zanesville to Cambridge, then on to the Pennsylvania state line.

When we traveled to Toledo, which we did every three months or so to see my cousins, aunts, uncles, Grandma and Grandpa, we would travel in the general north-west direction, taking a variety of county and state roads. It took FOREVER, as a child, to get to Grandma's house, where we stayed for the duration of the visit.

Grandma and Grandpa's home was a two-story brick house built in the late 1920's, with a full (creepy to me) basement, ground floor and an upstairs with the sole bathroom and three bedrooms and then, of course, an attic where one could walk upright due to the steeply pitched roof. My Sister and I slept in the middle bedroom which had a magical window that was a doorway to adventure! General Fairy Dustings, Halloween, Easter and especially Christmastime were a cause for wonder and excitement.

After Midnight Mass, sleepy headed children would go to bed. My Sister, my Muse of Imagination, was in charge of Christmas Eve Santa Sightings. She would tell Santa stories, interrupting occasionally with, "Did you hear that? Was that a hoof step on the roof?" Or, "Was that sleigh bells?" She would sometimes wake me up in the very cold dark of the Eve of Christmas to ask me these questions, sparking my imagination to the point of "YES! I hear it!"

Or, "I saw Rudolph's nose!" I would wonder at the time how Santa and the reindeer could possibly manage the steep roof without falling off, but I was confident in his magical ability to handle it all. Indeed, Santa and his reindeer HAD come in the long, dark, northern Ohio night to leave presents for all.

If you were raised in the Christian tradition, many of you can reach back into your memories of seeing or hearing Santa's sleigh or a glimpse of a fluffy white Easter Bunny tail. If you were a child raised in the Jewish, Muslim, Hindu, Buddhist, Indigenous or other faiths, most likely you can recall magical or spiritual experiences during high holidays. This is not an argument for or against the "realness" of Santa or other mythical or religious figures, but an invitation to explore the POWER of our minds and our imagination.

Our Deepest Soul Selves remember seeing colors, possibly images or people that others did not see. Our Deepest Soul Selves remember hearing sounds or music, or possibly a voice that others did not hear. Maybe even now, we experience these things and just brush them off, or push them down into the depths of our being where we have safely stored these experiences since we were little children. And maybe now, it is time to shake the cobwebs off those parts of us. Maybe now it is time to accept, explore and even celebrate that our Deepest Soul Selves can offer us a liberation we never knew we had; a freedom to love ourselves, our world and our lives in a fully encompassing way. Let's take a step together towards this new possibility.

CHAPTER 4
Your Invisible World

Every thing is a vibration be it a thought, a piece of furniture, musical passage, oil painting, gust of wind or a thesis paper. Every thing. Vibration equals sound equals frequency equals color equals number equals energy. Even every organ in our body vibrates or oscillates at a particular speed/frequency/color.

We used to be attached to the philosophy of "I'll believe it when I see it" and physical evidence was confirmed by our eyesight. Said philosophy went very badly for Galileo, a brilliant astronomist, physics mathematician, engineer and natural philosophist in the 16th and 17th century. Even though his work moved us into modern science, the Roman Inquisition visited him, not taking kindly to his work. The concept of the movement of heavenly bodies and his discovery the earth was indeed not flat nor stationary, was their primary objection. He spent the last ten years of his life under house arrest because he, well, told the truth. (Just for fun, check him out on Wikipedia because there is very cool stuff about him and his life that is pretty fascinating.)

A little more recently, Alexander Graham Bell, scientist, inventor and teacher of the deaf, opened a vast world of possibility by inventing the telephone in 1876. A disembodied voice from hundreds of miles away stunned the entire world and was nothing short of a miracle!

Now we use devices to have a profusion of information and communication at our fingertips, our voice, or even with a motion. We take for granted the ways in which these gifts are transmitted to us: radio waves, microwaves, electrical impulses, radiation and other forms of transmission, powered by a large variety of fuel sources. Most of us gladly use our cellphones, for instance, and we trust THESE transmissions, even though we cannot see them in our visual spectrum. These evidences, in solid, physical reality, started "life" as inspiration, invention, creativity.

For millennia, inventors and creators of art, music or science, found much of their inspiration (Imaginari, Inspiratio/Soul) in Dreamtime, be it actual sleep, meditation or deep musing wherein brain waves are observed to operate primarily in Alpha/Theta states. It is recorded that St. Teresa of Avila would levitate during her deepest hours of prayer and adoration and yogis around the world know this in their own practices. Many of us have seen potent outcomes with the power of prayer and what is prayer but the combination of thoughtform and emotion, the two most dynamic and encompassing creators in and of our lives.

Elementary School children have learned for decades that we are but a bunch of molecules moving slowly enough to be visible to our physical eyes. Quantum Entanglement finds that molecules can exist in two places at once. This is stunning! Ultimately, this means WE can exist in two places at once! This is only the beginning of realizing our true potential!

If you have not seen the documentary "What the Bleep Do We Know", I highly suggest it. It is, to me, where God and Science meet. In the film, they mention the work of Dr. Masaru Emoto who spent his life's work studying the effects of thought and prayer on water molecules. I had the honor of meeting him and attending a conference in Austin, Texas where he was a keynote speaker. There is much science in this film, and I must say it is quite eye-opening about the power of prayer and thought.

Before this book creates a reality show project where Superman meets Deepak Chopra, let's dial it back a bit and end this chapter with this: WE are powerful creators. We have seen and been given the signs our whole lives and possibly have chosen to play it "safe" and ignore the signs, or have not trusted our own sense of knowing.

You are reading this now because you have been guided by your own intuition, your deepest felt sense, your highest wisdom, to claim your right to your own power, inner strength and knowing. Your Deepest Soul Self can be your guide to remember that you are held in profound love and are not alone. Your Deepest Soul Self can show you the courage you already have to explore the possibilities in store for you.

CHAPTER 5
My Invisible Friends

I mentioned in Chapter 2 that I learned to soften my "veil" of awareness as a young girl, to enable more interaction with Earth Spirits. I introduce the concept of my "antenna" in this chapter. The distinction for me is "veil" is more of a visual nature, and using my antenna is where I actively reach out with a query and I receive an answer through an inner hearing of a word or words, a feeling, an inner picture or scene, a smell, a distinct "knowing", sometimes a sensation or any combination of these things. I remember beginning my queries after I started school at the age of 6.

Unlike remembering exactly the moment I flew, my awareness of my invisible friends came to me much like the learning of faeries, gnomes and other earth spirits; gradually. Those earliest experiences paved the way to discovering I had, what I shall call, an "antenna" in my awareness that I would sometimes raise, much like the earliest cell phones wherein we pulled the antenna out when we wanted to make or take a call. I am very aware today of stopping myself completely when I want an answer from my Deepest Soul Self about anything from what spices to use in a soup to what road to take. It actually feels like I open my mind up to receive "the signal" of input, advice or suggestion from what I know now to be one of my guides or possibly my own Deepest Soul Self. Sometimes I take the advice or not; it is totally my choice.

That sounds quite simplistic and I admit, strange to some, but from a young age I learned to feel into a situation, be it deeply and quietly observing the ladybug convention or stopping outside my 1st grade classroom to assess the environment within before gathering courage to enter. I learned to use either the veil opening of visual acuity and more readily from school age on, my antenna.

I was exceedingly shy as a little girl and would hide in my mother's skirts when we went into town. In the early 1960's, women rarely went into public wearing anything but dresses or skirts, and there I found a little safety. This excessive shyness leant itself well to encouraging my natural queries and observations of energies and the spirit world. In spite of the fact that my innate energetic tendencies had been stymied by my well-meaning parents to the point of not sharing my deeper self with them anymore, I feel that the actual development of these tendencies was amplified due to my dysfunctional home environment and early school years. Even though my parents loved us very much, they carried their own unhealed pain and it bled over onto us. The trauma I experienced from being exposed daily to both of these unsettled, unsafe and fluctuating climates caused my instincts for safety to became honed. I used my energetic gifts automatically and without fail.

I started school when I was six and my Sister and I traveled 45 minutes by school bus to arrive in town to attend Catholic school. We went to mass every morning in the historic, austere church and even though I went to mass every Sunday with my family, daily mass was a terrifying event for this shy, country girl. For three years, at the beginning of the fall school term, I dreaded everything about going to school because of my terror.

We sat in grades from 1st through 12th with the nuns who taught each class overseeing the behavior of their students. The first year I sat at the very front of the church with my unknown classmates and teacher, Sister Mary _____. I had never been in such close proximity to a mysterious nun in full habit, which was daunting. As the weeks went by, I grew less afraid of Sister because she was a kind and gentle person.

The life-size statues of saints placed around the sanctuary all sternly glared at me knowing sins of mine I anxiously did not. Jesus' expression, as he bloodily hung above me nailed to the cross, as well as Mother Mary's expression were of pain and deep sorrow and I knew I had something to do with that. Catholic inspired guilt and shame was already taking root in my mind's fertile soil. I was so very afraid and once I looked up at Jesus, also tortured and alone, I burst into uncontrollable tears, my wails echoing off the walls of the huge granite/stone church, interrupting the Holy Sacrament of Mass. Elise was in the back of the church with her 6th grade class. Every day for three weeks when the fear spilled over, my wails echoed uncontrollably throughout the church and Elise was allowed to come stand beside me to ease my fears and tears. My sobs subsided, knowing I would be safe.

2nd grade was more of the same with my Sister coming to my aid. My liquid fears lasted only two weeks or so. 3rd grade my cries lasted until Holy Communion each day and for about a week. Elise was not allowed to stand beside me as her teacher felt I needed to quit being a baby and to learn my lesson. The lesson I learned from this was to hide my fears and pain. Human consolation would not come and I was all alone.

There was much anger and violence in my home growing up. Out of the anger between my parents grew fear in us children, as well as the natural evolution of deep anger within my sister and I. All children inherently, or at least subconsciously, know they are due a loving and kind home. As time went on, my mother and father's arguing worsened. Mom was not a submissive wife and there was no question of physical abuse towards her, but the yelling between them and the verbal, emotional and physical abuse toward us was offered regularly. When Dad got home from work, we sat down to dinner never knowing if he would be explosive or happy, nor Mom's response. Mom was not as violent as Dad nor nearly as often, but she certainly instilled deep fear in me many times. Later we realized Mom was pre-diabetic and hypoglycemic. Her occasional rage was at times attributed to blood sugar imbalances; a perfect opportunity for deeply buried anger to release onto her children. In my teenage years when we lived in a suburb near Columbus, Ohio, our neighbors across the street told us that in the summer time, when the windows were open, they always knew when our family was eating dinner because the loud bickering traveled the neighborhood.

Our mercurial and volatile environment was known to many, although we had loving times also. It seemed normal to us and honestly this was the way many adults handled their stress in their family homes. A board for paddling, a switch we were sent to collect to subsidize our own pain, a flyswatter in a pinch or a backhand were offered regularly, and shame, despair, embarrassment, fear and anger were amongst our early childhood lessons.

Enter my invisible friends. When I was six I started realizing I had a few friends I couldn't see that helped me feel safer. At first I didn't distinguish between one or the other, just that they were mine. When I was unhappy or scared, I turned to them to make me feel better. My antenna would reach out, and there they were! It isn't that "they" did anything initially, they were just present with me. I assigned them roles, since this was my game and all about me! Not surprisingly, I made two of them parents and often two others were present and became the children. These assigned roles were obviously a reflection of my desire for a safe and happy home.

My friends went everywhere with me and came forth when I needed them. During times of extreme loneliness I would reach for them with my "antenna". When we traveled long distances, it was entertaining to create cowboy scenes outside the window, and of course all four of them were excellent riders! In these scenes, for variety, I would try to add more kids or friends to the family, but I could not hold them in my mind. They would fade away. Today, my sense of this is that my four friends were my guides and/or angels and the others were my mental creations. There was less attachment to them and I cannot recall any independent actions from them, e.g. On a long ride to Toledo, I would set a scenario and my little family would find things to jump, water their horses, stop for lunch when I was hungry, etc. Of course there was never a question of how they managed to keep up! The new ones I would create would just dissipate during the ride like a two-dimensional cartoon character. They could not hold my interest or my heart.

Not only during lonely times did I reach for my invisible friends. At home or at school, after each of the many and varied times of attack, as they truly were attacks on my sensitive nervous system, gentle nature, loving and generous heart and physical body, if I could, I would retreat to the outside where I felt safe amongst my nature companions. If I was at home and it was not possible to go outside, I would escape to Elise's and my bedroom to be silent and quiet and reach out for comfort from my invisible friends. It was always there and I was grateful.

I am sure many of you created your own friend safety-net as a child. Psychology certainly has chapters and verses of children creating their own safe internal terrain. What I must say here is that even now, medicine – science - theology is still studying distinctions between mind – brain - consciousness. What is "real"? The more we study the less we are able to separate or distinguish human experiences and processes. What is within is without and the question and answer lies in realizing that nothing is truly objective. Separation isn't real and everything is subjective. Which is why my conscious mind did not realize that there was an impending danger in our lives, but my soul and heart knew a menacing doom was already upon us.

CHAPTER 6
The Downward Spiral

The torture of my Sister began when I was five and she was 10 and continued until she was 15 when we moved to a suburb of Columbus, Ohio. Elise disassociated during the abuses and suppressed the events so deeply the memories didn't start surfacing until she was in therapy in her 30s. At that point she stopped teaching special education and focused her life's work on becoming a clinical social worker specializing in teens' therapy. The angrier they were the more fulfilling her work was and they loved her. She understood them, loved them, and they knew it.

The horrendous occurrences happened by perpetrators that none of us knew, and even though Mom and Dad's dysfunctional parenting left much to be desired, they would have given their lives to protect my Sister if they had only known.

Our home started changing because of these events. The anger between Mom and Dad amplified, spilling over to us and continuing for the rest of their marriage. The eggshells upon which Elise and I walked became more prolific, not knowing which way the wind would blow. On a good day, I could help Dad outside in his motorcycle shed in companionable father-daughter time or have fun on a ride with him. Other days I stayed away for safety. As I grew, my veil and antenna (my energetic sensing mechanism and my query tool) became more accessible and trusted.

The subconscious terror and rage that my Sister felt eventually manifested itself in Adolescent Rheumatoid Arthritis. I remember her wails of anguish as nightly she submerged her crippled, pain-racked hands into a roasting pan filled with hot paraffin wax. After several minutes it provided a temporary relief of her pain, but the initial heat on her inflamed joints was torment.

Her feet and hands became horribly disfigured and all of her joints stayed inflamed. Many years later, in 1996, she had surgery on her hands in Louisville, Kentucky at one of the best orthopedic hospitals in the country. They had never seen such disfiguration before and they had seen plenty. They broke many bones in both hands to reform them. The resultant healing pain was acute but normal for her and the results were rewarding because her hands were less disfigured and she had more use of them.

In those early years, however, not only was this the awkward, gangly, adolescent period of her life, but the disease affected her walk. Only one toe, her big toe, actually touched the ground. One afternoon, we were walking down the hill from our school as we sometimes did, to go to a family friend's work to catch a ride out to our country house. A group of high school boys and girls walked behind us that knew Elise because she was a freshman in 9th grade. They were cruelly laughing at her and mimicking her arduous gait. I was confused, embarrassed and angry at their mocking of my Sister. There was no ignoring their brutal behavior but we both just kept walking. I am positive my Sister had to deal with this shamefulness much of the time, but I never remember her telling Mom or Dad about it. She just achingly endured.

My creative, brilliant, beautiful Sister who guided and protected me through my early years, was now on a path of survival, and had little to give me. She still tried to soothe and distract me when the yelling ensued, but even that occurred less and less, as her anger and resulting raging began bubbling up and out at Mom and Dad and eventually me.

Our home was a hotbed of known and unknown trauma. My Mother and Father carried lifelong guilt about Elise's

ARA, always wondering what they may have done to cause it, because they did every known medical thing to help ease it. The summer of 1966, days after I turned ten and Elise was 14 nearing 15, our family drove to the Cleveland Clinic to have the best assessment and treatment available in the country. We arrived the first week of August, and as we drove through the dark and ravaged part of the city still in curfew from the days-long Hough Race Riots, my Father nervously exclaimed about the pitch-black streets and devastation around us.

As for me, I didn't feel nervous or scared. I don't even remember feeling my Dad's fear. I had eventually become able to shut myself down during the progression of my Sister's torture and subsequent disease. I was numb to keep from feeling. I didn't reach out for help from my invisible friends anymore and they were not an active or even known part of my life by the time I was nine. I had to block any sensation or deeper knowing I previously had in order to withstand Elise's suffering. As a matter of fact, I didn't realize how much I HAD shut down during this period of my life until my deep remembering in order to write this aspect of my story.

In the middle of my 5th grade, when I was 10, and Elise was 15 in her sophomore year, Dad got a job near Columbus, Ohio and we moved. I have many memories of this period of my life, and I am certain my angels and guides never left me, but my veil and antenna stayed deeply hidden within my being, because I could stand no more feeling, understanding or sensation than I was already experiencing in my life. It was many years before I felt their presence again. This didn't keep me, however, from living a life that brought accomplishments, fun and beautiful experiences.

Maybe you can relate to this need for protection. Maybe this is all that you remember feeling your whole life; being armored against the world. I eventually rediscovered what I had buried. I eventually remembered that love and divine help is never far away; as a matter of fact, it is fully present within and without us and reveals itself at the perfect time. If you are still armored against the world, you are, right now, in the perfect time and place.

CHAPTER 7
My Regular Life

Music had been a part of my life from a very early age. On Saturday mornings in the country outside of Zanesville, it was house cleaning time. Mother would put a ballet on the record-player and we would clean. From four years of age, I always had chores to do, even if it was only making my own bed and helping Sister clean our room. Music from Swan Lake, The Nutcracker or Sleeping Beauty would flow throughout our home, lifting my heart, body and spirit. This is where my love of music and dance began.

Every six months or so, a ballet would come to town, and from the age of six on, Mom would take my sister and me. I was enraptured! After the intermission, about half-way through the 2nd half of the presentation (or when I couldn't sit still any longer) I would tell my Mother I had to go to the bathroom. The first time, at six, she looked conflicted as she didn't want to miss the ballet and she wanted me to feel safe since I tended to be such a shy girl. I insisted it was ok to go by myself and after she confirmed I knew where to go and firmly telling me to come straight back, I was FREE! I went to the bathroom and then into the hall where no adults were about and began dancing! I twirled, ran, jumped and danced as the music floated out to me and I became airborne! I remember one year when an adult was in my dance hall and I was heartbroken because I was too shy to play ballerina in front of anyone!

We traveled in the car a lot as a family, and many times we sang; my Mother, Sister and I and occasionally, my Dad. Mom and Dad both had good voices, as did my Sister. "Down by the Old Mill Stream", "She'll Be Coming Round the Mountain", "Billy Boy", "Shenandoah", "Amazing Grace", "This Old Man", "I Love You, a Bushel and a

Peck", "3, 6, 9, the Goose Drank Wine", and every variety of Christmas music there was during the season, and the last resort "100 Bottles of Beer on the Wall" until my Dad couldn't take it any more.

After we moved to Columbus, Dad bought a "Hi-Fi" console and records from The Carter Family, Kate Smith, Patsy Cline, Glen Campbell (Dad's), Rubber Soul, Sgt. Peppers Lonely Hearts Club Band, The Rolling Stones (Elise's), Paul Revere and the Raiders and The Monkees (mine) took turns in the place of honor. I loved everyone's music and would play it as loud as I dared when Dad wasn't around. The first album I purchased was a gift for my Dad, the soundtrack to Patton, which I adored! I would take it into the band room in high school for my study hall because I was generally a good kid since I was too afraid to be bad, and was given unmonitored access to the room. I would loudly play it on the large sound system and absorb it. My band director was surprised when he found me there one day, enthralled, and I believe he had a new perspective of me and my music appreciation.

My sister and I were both musicians from a young age. Elise played violin and later fiddle for most of her life until her mid-30s, when the excruciating pain in her crippled hands became too much to bear for her to play. I played violin from age 6 to 10 and then picked up clarinet. After we moved, Mom and Dad continued our tradition of musical training such as we'd received at St. Nicholas in Zanesville which had a very large music program. They chose our new home outside of Columbus based on the school and its music opportunities. Elise went immediately into her 2nd semester of Sophomore year and played in the orchestra. I finished 5th grade and subsequently graduated 8th grade from St. Mathews Catholic School, taking private violin and then clarinet lessons while there.

When I began Junior High School as a 9th grade freshman, I had my first concert band experience, only having prior orchestra experience. Mr. Kessler, the Director of the Gahanna Lincoln Junior and High Schools' music program and the conductor/teacher, was known for fits of temper, regularly throwing things such as his baton or erasers. Most of the time the rest of the kids thought it was funny, however, I was never afraid of him. Male anger was nothing new to me and I loved him! His passion for the music and the knowledge he would share with us of the particular season and reason of history and the composer inspired me tremendously. From Mozart to Blood Sweat and Tears to Michael Jackson to Count Basey and Glenn Miller, I fell in love with everything about music. He opened a door of freedom for me I never otherwise would have seen.

Mr. Kessler actually changed the trajectory of my life as he watered and fertilized my passion for music. At one point in time, I truly considered running away from the craziness of my home to the point of starting to make plans, but I stayed because I could not imagine my life without the music.

When I graduated Gahanna Lincoln Junior High School and transferred to the High School, I lived for music. I played clarinet and then string bass in the orchestra, bass clarinet and then contrabass clarinet in the concert band, clarinet in marching band, tenor saxophone in pep band for basketball games, string bass in pit orchestra when we put on our annual musical and was the first girl in jazz band.

Until I came along, the jazz band was modeled on the Ohio State University all men's marching band. I approached Mr. Kessler when I was 16 about joining, and his reply was that girls were not allowed because boys had better rhythm. Upon hearing this my mouth dropped open and when I gathered myself, I incredulously said "have you ever been to a dance"? He saw my point. I taught myself baritone sax and enjoyed two years of big band music. We also had "contest" and played many solos for grading purposes.

Mr. Kessler recommended me to the Otterbien College's Music Director because they had an unused contrabass clarinet. I joined their concert band at 16. He continued to give me new musical challenges and since he was also the director of the professional Rockwell International Concert Band, I became their bass clarinetist also at 16, being the youngest member. Our tubist had been in John Philip Sousa's Band once upon a time and it was certainly an honor to play with this caliber of musicians. I played with them for four years.

Music fed me, soothed my soul and kept me sane during my growing up years. Dad's new job was a raise in status and money and Mom went back to work after the move. Even though we looked like a normal, now middle-class family and we had moved away from the torture situation my Sister experienced, it's years long tentacles were firmly entrenched throughout our family. Elise didn't start to uncover these events until she began her journey of self-discovery many years later, but the rage, confusion, fear and grief always lived beneath the surface of the oily waters of our family. Additionally, the guilt my parents felt in seeing their daughter suffer so, added another layer in the murky, thick soup of daily life in our household.

As Elise "acted out" more, surviving in the only possible way she could manage on top of her immense physical pain and the mental/emotional/spiritual damage done by the torture, our household violence continued. Mom and Dad's marriage was an epitome of dysfunction and Elise and I wished they would divorce. The physical violence was not between them, but Elise and I received irregular hits, slaps and pushes, enough to fear it at any time.

When I was 14, Saturdays were "hang out with the friends day" after chores were done. This was a snow-filled Saturday as Columbus usually was in the deep winter. Hoping to impress a new cute boy in the neighborhood, I decided to put on eye make up which I had never done before. In those days, "waterproof" mascara was brand new and I didn't have it yet. As usual, a rowdy snowball fight eventually ensued. When we were finally good and wet and cold we decided to walk over to one of the friend's houses for a round of hot chocolate and I went inside to let Dad know. He took one look at my face and slapped me in the head. With ears ringing, I shamefully told my friends I couldn't go and went upstairs to clean my face as ordered.

The ringing in my head dissipated overnight and I seemed a little different in choir at church the next day, but went about my Sunday as usual. I went to school on Monday and in basketball practice I realized my left ear felt different. It didn't hurt so I experimented with it, showing my teammates what I could do. At dinner that night, I said to my Mom and Dad "Look! I can breathe through my ear", pinched my nostrils and did just that! My parents were stunned, and then both realized what had happened. Mom angrily told Dad, who was shocked and shamed, that he would take me to the Doctor the next day.

As my father and I sat in the examining room with the Doctor, Dad's remorse was tangible and he told him the reason we were there. After examining me, the Doc said my eardrum was shattered and he wanted to allow it to possibly heal before considering reconstructive surgery. He explained this area of my body was the most sensitive part and it would hurt tremendously; I needed to sit perfectly still while he put a tiny piece of protective material in my ear. His manner was kind and gentle and he performed the task. The pain was excruciating and tears streamed down my face as I withstood the process. Dad's suffering equaled mine.

Today, the Doctor would have reported Dad to the authorities. Instead, we traveled home in silence with a 30 day sentence hanging over my head. We would go back in a month to see how much my eardrum was healed, if at all.

I do not remember my Father ever looking at me and saying he was sorry. He may have and I do not remember. It would have been such a tremendous, unprecedented moment though and I feel I would have remembered it.

I did not know at the time, but my Mother, who firmly believed in the power of prayer, reached out to her sister, my Aunt, who was a prayer warrior in her own right, and possibly others, to put me and my ear at the center of their healing prayers. I continued life as usual, staying off the basketball court for a while, but everything else at school stayed the same. I remember not taking showers but baths with Mom helping me wash my hair.

One month later, Dad and I were in the Doctor's examining room again. The first thing he did was remove the material, which hurt somewhat, but nothing like before. He looked again into my ear and then told us with an amazed smile that it appeared my eardrum was completely healed. He had never seen anything like it before. Dad told him, "Well, we've been praying."

I remember feeling shocked that my Father prayed for me. How else did I feel about this experience I had when I was 14? I know I was not angry at my Dad; he was so deeply contrite about how he had hurt me. How could I be angry? Additionally, I was shut down much of the time towards my own emotions during those years of my life from the torture of my Sister and the tragedy that prevailed in my family, it wasn't until I began opening again to my feelings and the spirit world in my early 20s that I began to "feel" again. I was numb to most of my own deep feelings.

I now understand I did my best to avoid feeling the feelings of others, but in fact, I felt theirs more than my own.

Throughout all those years after we moved to the Columbus area, I continued to use and escape into music allowing it to sustain me, letting it feed my soul. I was lucky and blessed to have it, and I am grateful my parents, especially my mother, who always saw to it I had the lessons I needed and the money for band camp and other functions. She regularly attended my concerts even though my father did not, which was a source of sadness for me for many years.

Even though I didn't have known access to my Spirit Partners who I used to call "my invisible friends" when I was a little girl, the healing vibrations of hearing and making music nourished me and the highs and lows during my Columbus years were like a volatile, exciting, fulfilling and confusing time of my life.

Unbeknownst to me, my psyche created layers of protection to keep me as safe as possible. I learned to function on top of the muddy waters of anger, pain and fear of my home, negotiating the battlefield whilst shining at school or church.

The layers eventually, gently, began unwrapping as life allowed. I became a little wiser, softened a bit, learned more and began opening, once again, to my Spirit Partners after I left my home and the felt sense of imminent danger wasn't battering me constantly.

If you feel you may have a few layers of protection or have had times of intense pain or fear in your life, know that it is always possible to come back to the purest sense of your self. Know that your precious light, your confident sense of well-being is still within you, secretly delights in and patiently awaits your letting go, and resting into the beauty that is your full self.

CHAPTER 8
Opening Doors

My Mother discovered Edgar Cayce when I was 13. I was in 8th grade in Catholic School when Mom started exploring this new world of spiritual possibility. She started meditating. Dad, being a staunch, old-school Catholic, was deeply disturbed by Mom's new passion and this was an immense cause of even more strife between them.

Edgar Cayce is called The Sleeping Prophet. He was born in and lived in Kentucky in his earlier years, was a devout Christian and had to overcome his moral struggles because from the age of 10 on he had trance experiences and other visions. In 1890 after a baseball injury, he fell into a trance and diagnosed himself and recommended treatment while in trance state. He became known as a medical clairvoyant and eventually in trance, also began speaking of past lives, Atlantis and reincarnation. He has been named as the father of the "New Age" movement in the western world.

First the book, *The Sleeping Prophet* appeared in the house, and then other books published by Mr. Cayce's organization, Association for Research and Enlightenment (A.R.E.) started appearing. I picked one or two up, being a voracious reader since early childhood. I read about re-incarnation, which made perfect sense to me. Mom never suggested I read the books and never brought any of the subjects up with me, unless I would ask her opinion on something I may have read.

This was the spark I needed to have hope in "something more". I even brought reincarnation up in school one day in Religion Class, when our Priest was visiting. He said, "Well, the Bible doesn't speak of it, but it doesn't speak against it." That was all I needed to move forward in my own tender life of inquiry.

I would like to say this was a breakthrough towards feeling my connection to rediscovering my Invisible Friends or Spirit Partners, with my "antennae" of inquiry, or even recapture the wonder and beauty of our magical friends living within the natural world. None of this happened. I had too many years of shutting myself off from my higher level of sensitivity and my inner knowing to protect myself best as I could within the dysfunctional and painful environment in which I still lived. I did not feel safe enough in which a natural opening could happen. I had lost my inner knowing of my Invisible Friends years before.

I loved God, however. Immensely and deeply. I prayed to God regularly, generally asking for help in certain matters. I had an innate knowing there was a God who loved me much more than I loved myself, and I remember often bartering with God when I was asking for help.

While I was keeping my last report card a secret which HAD to come out, my conversation with God went something like this: "PLEASE God, help me! Don't let Dad (or Mom) get so mad at me because of my D in Math! If you help me, I promise I will stop masturbating"! OR "God PLEASE make it better! I can't stand it anymore! The yelling and hitting is killing me! I promise I will be a better person!"

Well, the results of my D in Math were what they were, and possibly God eased some of the repercussions, and days or weeks later my curiosity about my body and budding sexuality got the better of me and occasional nighttime experimenting before sleep would once again happen, to my guilty pleasure.

I knew I had a Guardian Angel because I was taught that in Church and School, but sometimes I thought I might have two Angels. I knew they were around when God was busy with something else and I convinced myself they didn't get mad at me or disapprove as much when I sinned. Lying to Mom or Dad to "save myself" from their anger, seemed somewhat acceptable in the larger heavenly scheme of things. My Guardian Angel(s) job was to mainly keep me safe from things like getting hit by a car or strangers (I was never clear on that aspect).

Jesus? Well, I hadn't met Jesus yet and had no frame of reference in my heart about The Christ, even though we certainly had it drilled into us in in school and church. Years later when I was open to the possibilities of my spiritual nature as an adult, I occasionally had "conversations" with The Christ Jesus. I saw him not only in my mind's eye but in the palpable energetic sense of my third eye. The first time it happened, he unexpectedly appeared when I was in the middle of doing something and smilingly assured me a concern I had was not to be bothered with. I don't even remember the specific occasion or concern as this has happened periodically throughout my life. I will say my Jesus is a laughing Jesus and His energy/The Christos is very joyful and uplifting.

After discovering the possibility of reincarnation and realizing there is a bigger spiritual world than what I had known, the violence, fear and pain in my home life became easier to bear. Even though the deep joy and pleasure I had in my larger musical life in school as well as the heart openings I would have as I sang in our church choir soothed and eased the roiling of my spirit, the real ease came when my heart knew I was not alone anymore. Interestingly, it wasn't my one or two Guardian Angles I thought I had that caused me to not feel alone, it was the certainty that I had lived other lifetimes with other family and friends and communities. It was this connection to humanity that soothed my heart. Years later, learning and re-meeting my

Spirit Family became my solace, but reincarnation brought me my first spiritual joy.

My Sister left home when I was 14 and life was not as contentious. She came home from college when she had to, graduated with a degree in Special Education and then moved to New Mexico where my Aunt and Uncle lived. She returned home a few years later with a man who became her husband, and she taught in Kentucky for several years. A divorce, therapy and her heart led her to continue her education receiving her first Masters Degree in Clinical Counseling. Her own life's journey and her intentional unraveling of the tortures she endured as a young girl and the subsequent growing up years, set a fire within her to work with adults and teenagers having undergone such profound and possibly specific abuse as she had. My Sister's heart was a loving one, and being of service was her passion.

I left home at 20, after working two years in insurance at a large company in Columbus, Ohio. I moved to Kentucky to attend college but left after a full year. I did not have a major or a knowing of "what to do when I grow up" and decided I wasn't going to waste my Father's money nor my time. That was the "stated reason" as we say in marketing. The "real reason" is I wanted out from underneath my Dad's control and wanted to discover, well, myself.

Of course, this is a lifetime discovery, isn't it? I was accepted into a Telephony Central Office Installation training program; was the first and only woman in the program and I excelled. I was hired by the company and had two glorious years installing private phone systems into businesses in Kentucky. We were one of two private phone companies in Kentucky at the time and were competition for "Ma Bell". I was the only female installer in the private sector and possibly the whole state. A few years at this job and I found myself moving on, motivated by love.

Meanwhile, music? My Sister, who was living and teaching in Kentucky during these years, was playing fiddle instead of the classical violin she grew up with, and I taught myself guitar. We had fantastic jam sessions with fiddle, guitar, banjo, spoons, harmonica and folks bringing in other instruments occasionally, once even a trombone! Elise and I went to fiddle contests in Kentucky and Tennessee, never running into another female fiddler. I am sure there were women competing at the time, but in the late 1970's and early '80s, we were the only sister competitors I knew of. Did we win? Nah. We were pretty good and we had fun but the excellence of the Appalachian-raised musicians was stunning!

Those Kentucky years were filled with work I loved and music I adored. I was a free woman with a strong body from hard work and weightlifting and I was bold and fearless. What an exciting time to be young and alive! I discovered I could get a drink at the gay bar when I was only 20 as carding wasn't an issue then. I regularly closed the bar down, dancing by myself and was quickly accepted by the gay men.

When I was 21, I discovered pot and played with a little acid, as well as a tad bit of speed and downers. I didn't care much for the last three and my one attempt with cocaine left nothing to be desired. I enjoyed wild grown psilocybin mushrooms three different times Kentucky Style; once in squirrel soup, once on pizza and once on a hike deep into the Cumberland Mountains. Wonderful things grew wild in Kentucky!

The earlier love motivation I mentioned re-entered my life. He prompted me to move from Kentucky and the door opened more fully to my next stage of burgeoning awareness and spiritual adventure. My job at the telephone company was relocating to Atlanta and I was invited to move. I declined. My boyfriend, later my husband and I decided to pack up some things and move to California to start a new life together. He lived in Virginia and got his things in order and I moved back to Mom and Dad's in Ohio. As I always did during college breaks, I took a temporary job at a temporary employment agency to make and save money for our new venture.

My intentional research into my own gifts during this time was interesting and thrilling and caused me to start coming back home to myself. It is never too late and we are never too old to rediscover our essential, exciting natural gifts with which we were born. They are a blessing to us, sometimes in disguise, and are ultimately necessary to live a full, peaceful and vital life on this Earth.

If you are looking for that missing piece to the puzzle of your happiness and contentment, that missing puzzle piece may be your Deepest Soul Self and your connection to your true spiritual nature. Your discovery awaits.

CHAPTER 9
Stepping Through

Those three months back at home were exciting for me. I had a new adventure awaiting, a boyfriend both Mom and Dad approved of, an interesting temporary job at a major insurance company where I made a dear new friend and the most compelling piece was the full-on companionship with Mom. We shared hours of our thoughts and experiences of our spiritual lives, even taking a 10 week "Spiritualist" class which I will define as Psychic 101.

We attended the first once-a-week class and we found a small group of friendly, curious women in a neat, well-ordered home of C and S, the instructors. C and S were sisters and I recall the classes being fun and lighthearted as each week brought a new topic to experiment with. Before we began a class, C, who facilitated the most, would say a prayer of protection. There was always a feeling of safety within their home.

The first class was about "Psychometry". Each of us removed an item that we were wearing that meant something to us. A scarf, keys, a watch, bracelet or other various articles were deposited into a basket. After we had a seat, one of the sisters brought the basket to each of us and we selected something that was not ours. Putting the item into our left hand, which is understood to be the "receiving" hand, we spent a time quietly focusing on the object. After a short period, maybe 10 minutes, we then took turns sharing what we had perceived. There was no pressure or rush and each person had time to remember impressions they experienced. Images, if that is what we had, did not come fully or instantly, but in bits and pieces. After each share, the owner of the item would confirm anything the other would share if it fit. Surprisingly, every woman there had a few accurate things to say about their "practice" item.

An impression that was spoken about a piece of jewelry, for instance, went something like this: "I saw an older woman with white hair. She was cooking at a stove. Later there was a very tall man, and I saw a two story house. Cows. And horses? I felt sad. That's all I can remember now". The stated jewelry ending up being a ring that the woman's grandfather gave her grandmother on a very special anniversary. They were farmers and of course Grandma was a good cook. When she died, the ring went to her oldest granddaughter who kept it precious.

A couple classes focused on seeing and feeling our aura. Interestingly, this first "feeling" practice we also explored in Massage School nine years later. At the time, before the internet and the wonderful flow of research and information, the understanding was that the Etheric Aura, closest to the body, extended 5-6 feet out from the body. Auric layers have different colors to them and I know people who can see many colors and layers, but I have personally only seen other people's auras as white even though I sometimes now see my own auric colors.

The first exercise was a practice in feeling another's aura. We had a partner for this venture and we stood facing each other about 15 feet apart. We would each take one step towards the other and in the quiet, calm room notice if there was any felt sense of the other. We continued until we were only a few feet apart. There were as many varied results as there were people. Some of us felt the other quicker and some slower. There was no right or wrong here. I loved this experiment and could palpably feel the other's aura or energy field as a "thicker air" sensation. As we continued to get closer, it went from an "airy" feeling to "watery".

The next aura practice had us practicing seeing another's aura. A woman sat in front of an empty, light colored wall.

We all sat in chairs six or eight feet away from her in a semicircle. We then took a few minutes as we closed our eyes and focused on our breath in a calm manner. When we were ready, we looked at our new friend though half closed "soft" eyes, directing our gaze not on her face, but beyond or to the side of her face or body. It took a little time for me looking, closing my eyes again, looking again. I wanted to see so badly. I was trying really hard. Finally, after giving up and relaxing into the thought I'd never see it, there it was! A white glow around her whole body, looking like a full-body halo extending about 18 inches from her.

We all got a chance to be observed and to observed. Again, every experience was different. There was no judgment or explanations attempted as to why one of us could perceive and another could not. It was all new and because of the safe, loving atmosphere, we all came to be a support to each other exactly how we were.

Another partner exercise we did also included changing partners as the experience was different with each one. The experiment was mind to mind sending and receiving. Regardless of things you may have seen on shows and the internet, this was a rather simple practice. We would sit with our "Psychic 101" friend and we would take turns being the "Sender" or "Receiver". After all of us doing our usual set-up for class, a protective prayer, calm, mindful breathing, the sender would choose an "item" such as their dog, a car, a book, something singular and simple, and broadcast to their partner. When an image came into the receiver's mind they would say what the image was. If it was incorrect they would continue the exercise. Again, we had different results. Partners would switch their "sender/receiver" roles and play again.

The outcome was that each of us realized we generally were better at sending or receiving, not both. One can always practice, if they wish, to improve their lesser skill (as with any of these techniques), but for me, it has been shown over and over I am a much better receiver versus sender.

An interesting thing happened at work during this short time at home. It was a small thing really, compared to the regular occurrences I had as a child of interactions with magical things or "other world" friends. I was at the Xerox machine doing a long copy task which fell to me as a temporary employee. As I stood there, paying only half attention to the simple, boring job, I became aware of an energy or entity a few feet away. It was not "standing" on the ground. It was largish as an auric being would be (having that frame of reference from feeling auras in my Psychic 101 class). I didn't see it as a color or being, but "saw" it with an awareness only. I felt nothing from it probably because I was still quite shut down emotionally from my childhood traumas. It could have been, and maybe was, emanating loads of love towards me, but I didn't feel it. I remember, however, being a little freaked out and not knowing what to do. I started saying the "Our Father" as Catholics call the "Lord's Prayer" and continued to do so as I completed my task taking full, calming breaths. By the time I got back to my desk it was gone and I just continued with my day.

As I look back on the incident now and go back to my earliest experiences of "feels" or intentional openings, I recall I had my "veil" of awareness. This was more of a visual nature in seeing energetic beings, which I now know were real but not in our dimension. My other tool I developed a little later was my "antennae" of inquiry where I would reach out with a question or maybe a request for help, protection or simply company when I was afraid or bored. Both of these tools or abilities shut down as the trauma and abuse increased in my life, AS FAR AS I KNEW.

Using this reminder for a frame of reference, I would say the class I was taking started developing intentional openings of my inner knowing, my 3rd eye. It gave me an opportunity to have choice in the matter of my explorations and choose to use my "veil" of awareness when I needed or wanted to, and my "antenna" when I was inquiring.

I also think there was the aspect of inquiry in general. This was new to my adult self, not having taken time at this point in my life to delve into my earliest seeing and energetic experiences and really track them to identify what was happening. I stayed away for years from that question because one can't dive into childhood realms without being willing to be honest and deal with the pain and trauma in order to heal one's self.

So my class opened up, in an exciting way, these possibilities and I likely was a mini-walking-inquiry all the time. No real awareness or control of the antennae aspect but I was curious and willing. I now know the entity was in fact one of my guides making itself vibrationally available for me to see in my limited but somewhat open state; it was a gentle nudge in the right direction of information and experience gathering of the possibilities of more love, more creativity, more freedom, more laughter, more of a life that I inherently knew was there for me.

Soon it was time for me to leave for California with my boyfriend, before the weather turned hazardous and unpredictable, so I would miss the last couple of classes. In order to not miss the past-life regression exercise, I was the first to experience this extraordinarily educational and fun adventure.

CHAPTER 10
New Worlds

As usual, shortly after we all arrived, we started with our opening prayer of protection and spent a few moments in calm, mindful breathing. We moved into a small room that was cozy and I lay down on the carpeted floor. The other ladies, Mom included, sat in a respectful semicircle around C and I. We had been coached in the process of this being a "power of suggestion" hypnosis, meaning, we would be cognizant at all times and could stop the process any time we wished. I felt no trepidation and in fact, was curious, calm and open to the exploration. I peacefully waited with eyes closed

C began by reminding me in her gentle, soothing voice that I was safe and protected at all times and I would observe the events in a detached, loving manner with no emotion, as all souls involved are safe. She asked me to see a space capsule in front of me. This was easy as I grew up with Apollo missions and in 1980, they were fresh in my imagination. She then asked me to step inside and close the door, making myself comfortable. C gently invited me to allow myself to travel to the first lifetime my soul wished for me to see. She then asked me, when I was ready, to step out of the capsule and look down at my feet to see what I was wearing on them, if anything.

I had tall sandals on such as I'd never seen. The soles were rather thick, the rest of the shoes were very soft leather and wrapped up my legs. They were more closed than open as sandals normally are. I was wearing a white robe or dress, sitting in a portico or garden area protected from the sun. I was surrounded by children playing; some were mine, some were the slave women's children. The land was a semi-arid rolling terrain and I could see I was living in a

54

large compound with eight-foot light-hued walls with a large wooden gate. I knew there was another wooden gate also tall but narrow, somewhere else in the wall. We were atop a hill or plateau. There were Roman Soldiers inside and outside the compound and many other people, mostly slaves, working the gardens, at the well, repairing the walls around the large gate, tending the livestock; a slaughter was taking place. All was normal activity and a general atmosphere of prosperity and well-being was present. There was a large, low house made out of the same material as the compound walls and atop the house was a perimeter walkway and a tower.

C then asked me to go forward a few years. My husband was home; a wealthy, high ranking Roman Officer. I understood as I observed the scene, that he would come home from his duties every several months to few years. I would become pregnant, easily it seemed, and he was pleased with me. I knew we were very fond of each other.

C then asked me to move forward to my death. I was an old woman and laying in my bed. Some of my children were around me. My husband was not there and I knew he had been killed in a battle a few years before. There was nothing spectacular about this scene. Just a natural outcome from the life I had lived. I was not afraid to die.

A note of interest: In college, I had an obsession with taking ancient Anatolian-related history, and in my Ancient Greek and Mesopotamian History classes, I had an irrational disgust for Alexander the Great, even emotionally blurting out to my professor "he was an egotistical asshole". It is my best thinking that the above incarnation was as a Roman woman living in Roman Turkey. In 334 BCE Alexander conquered the Persian Empire including Turkey, and then 190 BCE Rome invaded and conquered Turkey.

Continuing on, I was then asked to step back into my time capsule and travel forward to the next lifetime my Soul wanted me to see. When I was ready, I stepped out and looked down at my feet. I was wearing thinner sandals and standing outside what I think was my home. I was wearing, once again, a white tunic or dress. I looked at other homes built all around me and they were white or very light colored and we were on a mountainside.

I could smell the sea. I knew it was deep blue and that I loved swimming in the sparkling water. I was a young woman, 14 or so. C asked me to go into my home and go sit at the table for dinner. I went down the steps into my home and it was cooler as it was partially submerged in the ground. All along the walls down the steps and into the hallway was beautiful cobalt blue colors as well as other bright colors. I do not know if they were tiles of some sort or simply painted on and into the walls. At the table were many people, all jovial and I believe they were my immediate and extended family which included a family slave or two such as my beloved nurse. C asked what we were eating, and at this time of this writing, I only remember fish and not any other dishes. My sense is we were wealthy.

C then asked me to go forward in time a few years and I did. I was outside again but was not in my body, as it were; I observed massive devastation over my whole city, and saw grey everywhere. Everything was dead and the steps going down into our home were nearly full of ash. I went into the house and it was grey everywhere from the ash and death. Interestingly, I was not emotional, I was just observing and very curious.

Another note of interest: I am confident this home was buried in 79CE by the eruption of Mt. Vesuvius. When researching for this book, I learned Pompeii building materials were sometimes of a red substance. As I extended my research, I found there were a few neighboring cities that were buried only with ash, killing all there, unlike Pompeii which had ash, lava flow and pyroclastic material (also bringing death to everyone in the city). Herculaneam seems to fit my image of the town I lived in. Herculaneum was smaller and more prosperous than Pompeii and it was a resort city for wealthy Romans. Light marble was often used as some of the building materials and the blue materials in the wall mosaics I saw were more precious and used mainly in Herculaneum. I will discover the answer to this mystery when I am no longer using this body.

Continuing on my journey of the past, I climbed back into my time capsule to explore more of my soul's history and traveled forward in time. This took only an instant by now as I was familiar, eager and alert. I knew I could stop this exploration at any time but definitely did not want to.

When I stepped out I do not now remember if I looked down at my feet and if I did, what I was wearing on them. Again I was a young woman, maybe 15 or 16, beyond a reasonable marriage age. I was standing at the edge of some cliffs with the winds whipping my hair and the waves below wild and crashing. I looked around and saw my family home, a rectangular shaped castle with a second story on part of it and two turrets. There were few trees and the land was bleak and forlorn. Or I felt forlorn. I was deeply unhappy and longing for my love to come home from the wars so we could marry and I could leave this dark, unhappy life. I moved ahead in time.

I saw myself, wild with grief and anguish, throw myself from the cliffs to my death. I was aware my lover had been killed in the War, and I heard in my head the word "Roses". (I later felt with certainty this lifetime must have been during the War of the Roses, which was from 1455 to 1487 in England.)

On C's suggestion, I climbed into my capsule again, traveled forward and stepped out to look down at my feet. I was wearing dirty, heavy leather boots with laces. I was a man. I looked around and saw my fence line on prairie land and a low profile sodhouse. I knew I was a farmer and I had a little cattle. When my new wife and I first arrived, I had a milk cow, some kind of bull and two oxen that had pulled our wagon to this place. I was rich. Now, I had only an old milk cow and one oxen, the bull and oxen having run off. I had a 12 year old boy and a lazy wife; both huge disappointments. My heart was cold and I was mean.

I moved forward in time, and looked around. The fence was falling down, the house was collapsing on one end, and the whole prairie was yellow with dust. My wife was dead, as I'd killed her with work and cruelty and my boy left as soon as he was able. I had nothing to live for and and would soon leave behind this bitter life.

As C asked me to get into my time capsule again, she suggested I go several miles above the Earth and look down to tell what I saw. I did so, and when I looked down I burst into sobs. There were wars everywhere and I felt anguish over seeing and knowing it. She gently asked me to keep my eyes closed, focus on my breath and to become fully present in the room knowing I was safe, loved and protected. I gradually opened my eyes. Everyone was respectfully quiet and waited for me to speak.

I felt calm, grateful, excited at this new information and possibilities of learning more about myself. I took my cassette tape of the regression, said goodbye to my fellow travelers, and left with Mom, never to see these women again.

There were many times in my life when something else, a "new memory", would pop into my mind unbidden that was from a lifetime I explored. I never romanticized this knowledge, it just seemed interesting. In the history of our world, there were only a very few souls on this planet at any given time that were fortunate enough to be wealthy, much less famous, as some people like to glamorously think. Most of us often starved and lived in poverty. This experience left an open door to explore my life in a different way. In the years that followed, I discovered three of my significant others played a part in previous lifetimes; one in my Roman Turkish life experience and another in a Celtic lifetime, and the other in two different lifetimes in Great Britain.

As my understanding grew, I would come to realize events or behaviors I had in a past lifetime contributed to this current lifetime and it was a learning for me to break free of a behavior within a situation. It could be a repetitive pattern within a workplace that was unsatisfactory or a relationship with a lover that wasn't the healthiest and I would have a breakthrough (sometimes a slow-growing one) on the how and why of my behavior. It would be a freeing discovery like a "take a big, deep breath" or a satisfying "ah ha!" marvel.

Have you ever met someone that you felt you already knew? Have you ever had a series of events that happened as if by coincidence? A sweet feeling of serendipity? A sense of familiarity to a situation or place, a déjà-vu? Have you ever had an answer to a question you didn't know you had, or maybe an answer without even knowing the question?

These are all real things, nothing to disregard. Your Deepest Soul Self is trying to guide you into a better knowing of yourself, possibly gently directing you onto a different path that may take you into a profoundly satisfying life-journey.

So pay attention. Pay attention to the signs, feelings, nature's nudges, and stop, breathe, be grateful and listen. Your Soul has some sweet things to say to you.

CHAPTER 11
A New Life

I took my first train ride from Cincinnati to Alexandria, Virginia, and my boyfriend, Jacky, and I left in November of 1980. He had never been west of the Mississippi and I had, in camping trips with my family, but this was an altogether new adventure. Our plan was to stop in Roswell, New Mexico, because my Mom's Sister, Willa, (remember the prayer warrior and my busted ear drum?) and her husband lived there. They had an empty duplex and we settled in to stay until after Christmas before heading out to California.

In a nutshell, the engine in our car blew up shortly after we arrived and even though Jacky rebuilt the engine, it took enough reserves of our "new move" money that we then didn't trust we could go on to California to transition safely. Shortly after the new year, I interviewed and got a job at the Police Department in the records department and later as a dispatcher, and Jacky at Mercedes Benz as a mechanic. We settled in even more into our duplex and decided to get married in May, a few short months after landing in New Mexico. I was 24.

Our new life grew into one we loved. We had decent jobs, a sweet, cheap place to live, family I loved and new friends. Roswell was a small town then with very few motorcyclists, especially compared to now, and we made friends with the local bikers, including a few of the local chapter Banditos.

I had ridden on the back of my Dad's bikes from childhood although my first motorcycle experience was with my Uncle, Aunt Willa's husband. It was a thrilling day in Tennessee when he placed me in front of him on his Indian Chief for my very first motorcycle ride. I was two years old. I got both my drivers license and motorcycle endorsement when I was 17 and always make sure the endorsement transfers with my new drivers licenses.

After we decided we were making Roswell our home instead of forging ahead to California, Jacky brought out his vintage BMW motorcycle from Virginia and built me a custom 1965 Triumph Thunderbird as a wedding present. It was a striking canary yellow 650cc motorcycle that fit me like a glove. From daily local riding to longer rides on the weekend up into the nearby Sacramento Mountains where we would often stop in Ruidoso or Riverside for a couple of beers and a game of pool. Many times I rode alone, loving the freedom and beauty of it all. I never saw another woman riding her own motorcycle at the time in Roswell, and I usually wore my brightly colored leg warmers so they could be seen above my Friar boots. I was proud and didn't want to be mistaken for a man since I nearly always wore a helmet and riders were assumed to be men in those days. The annual fall motorcycle festival in Ruidoso, then called Aspencade and now called Aspenfest, saw other women riding their own bikes and we always acknowledged each other for the rarity we were.

I was young and this was the '80s folks! My life looked a little like this: I would get off from my midnight shift at 7am, sit out on the porch steps drinking a couple of beers and smoking cigarettes. Since I drank coffee all night it took a little while to unwind. I would eventually go to bed to sleep best I could. Depending on what shift I worked, I would be back at work at 4:30pm or 8:30pm. Weekends were definitely time for partying, and I'd discovered I liked smoking pot after all! I smoked regularly and sometimes heavily for about nine years until I quit completely.

This was a very intense, active life with a high stress job I loved and a marriage that saw my husband nearly killed in a very serious motorcycle accident. He took my motorcycle out on a test run one evening after doing some work on it and a drunk driver turned left in front of him. While he was unconscious on the street, another drunk ran over him. I was actually dispatching when the call came in. This caused a huge life change for both of us. He eventually healed enough of the traumas of his body, mind and spirit and today has a successful veterinary practice.

Having learned zilch skills to handle my emotions, I stuffed them well by drinking, smoking cigarettes and pot as well as having excessive amounts of caffeine and sugar, powerful drugs in their own right.

During the early days of our move there, I continued my "sending and receiving practice" with a friend from my old Psychic 101 class once a week or so. Through that basic practice I learned that I was consistently a better receiver than sender. Even now I find that to be true. I used to work very hard when praying for someone or sending them specific healing thoughts and energy. About 20 years or so ago, however, I got some brilliant advice from a good friend who is an Intuitive Practitioner. My friend suggested I pray, holding the particular thoughts and outcomes I wished for the person, and then release my prayers to my own Deepest Soul Self which would then send the healing energy to the person's Soul Self, which would basically then "download" the healing prayers or energy into the energies of the body/mind. Soul works easily with other Souls for healing and I still work with my own prayers and intentions in a similar method.

Being a person who receives easily has been a journey of its own. Whether we know it or not, all of us are receiving thoughts and energies from others, be it family, friends or in a larger mass consciousness scale. This can be quite overwhelming sometimes, even when we don't realize this is the cause of our overwhelm. We all can learn tools to keep ourselves sane, grounded, compassionate and loving. Alternatively, maybe we are the great "senders" and don't even realize it. There is something here to be learned in being accountable and responsible for our own energies and how they land on others.

Both of these scenarios are mine at any given time, and it is an ongoing learning in my journey. There are many resources out there to support your journey in this learning. For now, if you haven't already, immediately take the advice I gave you at the end of Chapter 2: sit down by a plant, calm yourself with your gentle, full breathing, notice the beauty of the plant, be grateful for the moment. Relish these small opportunities, maybe a few times a day. Expand on those moments and you will find there is Magic there for you to discover.

CHAPTER 12
War Movies

When I was a little girl, between five and nine years old, my family would regularly drive to Grandma and Grandpa's in Toledo, Ohio for a visit. Saturday afternoons and sometimes Sunday afternoon if it was a long holiday and Dad didn't have to go back to work the next day, were television time. (Remember, I grew up "outside" and TV was a special occasion.) This meant Dad and his Dad, my Grandpa, watched war movies, as in the early to mid-1960's WWII movies were very popular. Dad had been in World War II in the Army Air Corp and Grandpa had been in the Army in World War I. As a matter of fact, Grandpa and his brother were two of the very few men left alive in his unit, surviving the 1918-1920 Great Influenza Pandemic. So war movies it was!!

Being a shy and tenderhearted girl I was easily influenced by movies (still am, actually) and I could rarely watch a movie without being highly affected. The monkeys, witch, guards, trees and doorkeeper in *Wizard of Oz* were awfully scary to me, for instance, and the popular black and white science fiction weekly show, *Lost in Space* gave me nightmares. Mom would forbid me to watch the show, but I managed to sneak in to join my sister whenever I could because I loved science fiction.

Whenever we visited Toledo, however, Mom, Grandma, and most times Dad's sister, Aunt Lona were in the kitchen cooking, talking and preparing the large afternoon dinner we would have during those visits. (I never saw a man cook in his home while I was growing up.) It was a wonderful time for the women to catch up. The men, cousin Bob, myself and once in a while my sister watched the movie of the day.

Halls of Montezuma, Three Came Home, The Desert Rats, Sink the Bismarck, Two Women, The Guns of Navarone, The Longest Day, The Great Escape, PT109, Battle of the Bulge, The Dirty Dozen, The Train, Thirty Seconds Over Tokyo, Sands of Iwo Jima and *Bridge On the River Kwai* all captivated me. My eyes were glued to the current conflict and I wouldn't tear myself away for anything.

The most impressionable were the aviation themed movies: *Twelve O'Clock High*, *Flying Leathernecks*, *Wing and a Prayer* and *Flying Tigers* all made my heart soar! Mom, hearing the ongoing loud battle sounds pouring from the living room, would come from the kitchen with a raised voice to be heard over the noise "MELVIN! How can you let her watch that stuff!!! Marisa, go play! Find your sister!" I would sadly leave and sneak back in as soon as it was safe.

I grew up around airports. Dad excelled at his work and was brilliant with electro-mechanical, electrical and vector/signal usage so much so that he was used in a World War II secret mission, which I share in Chapter 24. My first memory of an airport was in London, Kentucky, where I flew (without wings) as a toddler. Dad worked at the London-Corbin Airport.

Later, he worked at the Zanesville Municiple Airport which was two to three miles down the hill from our country house. I went up in my first plane (with wings) at three years old with Dad piloting us in a Piper Cub: Mom, terrified of heights, Terese interested and wee me thrilled beyond all measure! Dad was accepted into the Federal Aviation Administration while he was there and eventually retired from the FAA. I went to work with Dad regularly, played with the elevator and watched the occasional airplane, nearly always single engine, land or take off.

When we moved to Columbus, Ohio, in 1966, we lived a short distance from Port Columbus International Airport, now named John Glenn Columbus International Airport. Rickenbacker Air National Guard Base, now called Rickenbacker International Airport, had shared usage of the long runways. For years, the excessively loud sound of a landing jet's reverse thrust was music to my ears, and when sleeping it never woke me up. The Base had an officers club which we enjoyed because of Dad's GS rating. The Base also had regular air shows and from the age of ten I was happily exposed to lots of air traffic and exciting aviation history.

The large shows had several World War II aircraft in great shape, most of them USA bombers, fighter planes, an occasional British fighter plane or two and a Japanese Zero or a German Luftwaffe aircraft. I was honored to see the first public display of an F-15 which was the first US fighter that could fly perpendicularly; straight up like a rocket immediately after takeoff. "Top Gun" old school much less Top Gun: Maverick (yes I'm a huge fan) makes this kind of flying common to everyone, but being present for this first impressive flight caused my patriotic tears to flow.

All of this background is to say I have had an unusual relationship with aviation from a very young age. Even now, every time I hear an aircraft in the sky, I try to locate it and see if I know what it is. After landing in New Mexico, I soon realized the deeper story behind my passion for anything with wings.

My Aunt Willa was psychically gifted in many ways, although she kept most of her skills and knowledge to herself. Shortly after arriving in New Mexico, she and I set up a regular time we would get together to meditate or practice some of my Psychic 101 skills. We played with psychometry, sending and receiving and past life auric readings. Similar to positioning yourself against a blank, light wall to see the aura, the reader/observer will wait and will sometimes see another face, or a clothes change, or even feel the energy change of the person they are observing. This is generally a past incarnation of the person that is appearing.

Aunt Willa and I agreed to try this one day after we meditated. We, of course, said a prayer of protection as we always did. I read her first, but honestly do not remember much about what I saw because my reading from her was astonishing.

I sat in the chair in her small, comfy living room. The sun shone brightly in as it does most times in New Mexico, so there were no lights turned on in the room. I closed my eyes and breathed slowly and calmly. She told me she saw a boy, maybe 17 years old. I was wearing a leather helmet of sorts, a leather jacket and a scarf around my neck. She saw an explosion and fire over me.

When she said the last words, a memory immediately surfaced from this lifetime. I was an English pilot and yes, I was 17 years old. It was early in the war and I was hit by enemy fire and my plane exploded. I remember being sad as I had had very few missions and felt I had failed in my duty towards King and Country. I thought of my mother and sisters as I died.

I told Aunt Willa my memories and said I had always wondered if I had lived during World War II because of my unusual interest in it. I have learned since that many souls reincarnated rather soon that had left during the war even though sometimes it is centuries before another incarnation. I also recognized why I have an illogical fear of lighting gas pilot lights.

This experience was certainly food for thought, and set the groundwork for the "fleshing out" as it were, of one of the lifetimes I experienced in my past-life regression in my class as well as another one that arose during my massage school experience.

Know that those strange recalls, foibles, odd things you like or don't like may have nothing to do with this current lifetime, but another. There is no right or wrong in these occurrences but paying attention to the signals, information or curiosities may be beneficial, especially because it is possible your Higher Soul Self may be trying to guide you into a wiser way of living.

CHAPTER 13
The Leap of Faith

My husband was a very analytical, nuts and bolts kind of man, being of German/Hungarian descent, and I learned to share very little of my thinking or experiences in these matters with him. I didn't realize that not sharing did nothing to promote intimacy in a relationship, but what did I know about intimacy and honesty? On our fifth wedding anniversary, we quite proudly bragged to our friends that we had never had an argument. I didn't understand at the time the sidelong glances but we were young and ignorant in the ways of relating in a relationship. When we got married we agreed at the time that if it didn't work out, we could just get a divorce. Not the best traveling papers there.

A few years into our marriage, my Aunt Lena, Mom and Aunt Willas's sister, died. Still studying occasionally with Aunt Willa and listening to the sharing of her experiences with "Spirit", I surreptitiously kept the possibility of my veil thinning, knowing Aunt Lena might come to visit. One night while sleeping in bed with my husband, I awakened to see her at the foot of my bed. Again, I saw her in my mind's eye, not my physical eyes as some do. I just knew she was there. The feeling faded and the more I strained to see, the less certain I was I had seen anything. I eventually went back to sleep.

I awakened the next morning and doubted if what I saw and felt was real, but I knew I needed to go back for the funeral. Though we were pretty broke at the time, having plenty of doctor bills from Jacky's accident, I went the 1500 miles and was so very glad I did. My sister, our three cousins who had lost their mom and I spent as much time together as we could. We shared stories and our similar thinking that it is possible to get visited by our dear ones after they depart. We had all been raised by women who had their own childhoods influenced by women and men raised in the South with Irish Scottish heritage as well as touches of Cherokee. The veil was spoken of, a caul over a newborn's face indicting they had the "gift" and magic, although the word wasn't used, happened often. These conversations usually happened quietly among the women. Elise and I had an agreement that whoever went first would visit the other one and make sure they knew they were being visited (and yes, later I definitely knew when Elise was around).

We spoke of these things. One of my cousins had a baby boy that was the first born grandchild and the apple of my aunt's eye. As much as my cousin was saddened that her son wouldn't grow up with his grandma, we knew Aunt Lena would always stay close and keep an eye on him. We four women cousins were in the grocery aisle as we were shopping for the baby when we spoke that last statement, and three of us saw a jar of baby food lift OFF the shelf, fall out and down leaving shattered glass and baby food on the floor. We looked at each other in amazement and started howling with laughter! The baby's Grandma was in agreement! At their house, where we stayed for a few days during the funeral, there was a plethora of lights going off and on with no one touching them during the time we all were there. A radio did the same thing a couple of times. We knew Aunt Lena was telling us she was fine and that she loved us and would always be there for us, especially her children and grandchildren, whenever they needed her.

Upon coming home, I resumed my work life, my marriage life as it were, and started pursuing my interest in healing through massage. I had a friend who had been trained and certified years before in Wisconsin. This was several years before state or national certification or licensing was coming into play. She taught me everything she knew and I received sessions from the only other local therapist. I gave massages to my medical doctor friend and with only a few coaching points and a business license, my friend and I hung our shingle up and officially began our massage practice together. Masseuse was the term used then and we had our work cut out for us keeping things in the "therapeutic" sense for some of the clients that came our way.

I eventually quit my job at the police department as I fell in love with the work and the possibilities of helping others in this way. I had plenty of clients referred to me by my doctor friend and I had all the work I wanted. I noticed that after working on someone with lower back pain, my low back would be sore; or when helping someone with neck and shoulder pain suffering from headaches, I would experience the symptoms after the session.

At about this time, my husband got a job in the Socorro area and I decided to go to massage school in Santa Fe. In 1989, I investigated massage schools in the state and chose The New Mexico Academy of Massage and Advanced Healing Arts, later named The New Mexico Academy of Advanced Healing Arts. The school is no longer in existence as Covid made it unviable to stay afloat.

In my massage school exploration excursion, I received my first channeled reading. A trusted friend had referred me and I was excited and a little nervous. The channeler was a sweet, quiet spoken woman who explained she channeled a group called The Guides. She assured me she was aware the whole time of what was happening during the reading and could stop at any time and she also assured me I may stop at any time. She got comfortable on a chaise lounge and I on a chair. We began after thirty seconds or so.

Her voice changed and a deeper, well-projected voice began: "May all beings be happy and free from suffering.

71

We bless this beloved one come today and we are honored and grateful for this opportunity to be of assistance. How may we serve you?"

Well, I started crying. I had a heavy heart and even though I rarely cried at the time, I felt so very safe and loved with those opening words and the tears flowed. My first question was about my sweet red Doberman who had been hit by a car a few weeks before when I was not home. According to the animal control who had picked her up, she had suffered before dying. This was a guilty anguish for me. The Guides said she transitioned easily with help from my and her guides as well as a grandfather ancestor of mine. She was happy and peaceful and wished no dismay for me, only love. They went on to tell me we had been together in a Temple to Artemis in Ancient Greece. I was a virgin Priestess and she was my deer familiar. The interesting thing about this is that I used to take Azteca camping with me often and I always put a red bandana on her neck because she looked so much like a deer, I didn't want her getting shot by a hunter.

The only other thing I remember now about the session is when I asked if I would be an animal bodyworker someday and they said if I wished, yes. But I must first learn and spend time with the healing practices with humans. I don't remember much else now about this session. I left, grateful in my heart for the help and felt a loving rightness of things in my life.

Shortly, Jacky and I packed up and put our house on the market. He moved to the Socorro area and I moved to Santa Fe to begin school. I went to school five days a week and on Friday afternoon would drive to Roswell, set up my massage table at Mom and Dad's and work on clients. Sunday afternoon I would drive to Socorro and stay overnight with Jacky. In the morning I would leave at 6am to make it to 8am meditation, a required class in my course, to begin my school week. When student clinic started, I would work in the clinic Fridays and drive that evening to Roswell, work there, drive to Socorro and drive to Santa Fe. 496 miles nearly every weekend.

I was committed, I was dedicated. When I tried to share some of the things I was learning about the body/mind/emotion connections to my pedantic husband he dismissed any relevance to the true nature of things. Admittedly, he came from a medical background in that his father had been a well-loved physician who worked for the Veterans Administration and there are many Viet Nam vets grateful to him. I knew, however, I was moving into a rapidly changing and relevant world for me, my heart and my soul.

We both realized the time was coming and agreed we would separate our paths, knowing we would divorce several months down the road after my massage school graduation. With this knowledge, I was now free to step in to the full extent of exploration and learning. I could never have imagined at the time what that would look like. This next stage of my life catapulted me into my desire to learn about sensation and sensitivities, my vision, internal and external, my abilities to use all the gifts I was developing at the time in order to assist people in their healing journey. Like my sister, I too, wished to do all I could to help others in the best way I knew how.

CHAPTER 14
Diving into the Deep End

I lived in a shared house with two other students from my school that was within walking distance to the school and downtown Santa Fe. I fell in love with the city as most people do who go there, so much so, that there was an inundation of folks who quit their well-paying jobs and established lives to live in Santa Fe's high cost of living. There were many a PhD waiting tables at any of the excellent restaurants in order to explore the healing Mecca that was Santa Fe. I was one of the myriad of people called to the area to explore the opportunities there.

In my fabulous school I was either immersed in or introduced to: Massage Therapy, Jin Shin Do, Medical Massage, Ortho-Bionomy™, Polarity Therapy, Meditation, Sports Massage, Trigger Point Therapy, the Trager Approach and during final testing week, Feldenkrais Method and Alexander Technique were also introduced to us. Every day we touched and were touched which was a profound and unusual thing to most of us. We learned to get comfortable getting naked in front of other people, in a respectful atmosphere of course, and at the end of every massage class, we would circle up and have a process/discussion time. We were on a table receiving or giving some form of bodywork nearly every day.

A normal week went something like this: 8am Meditation, Monday, Wednesday and Friday Massage class, with Anatomy and Physiology on Tuesday and Thursday. Every A&P class began with a guided meditation where the instructor took us into our bodies presencing us to our latest topic. Physiology was the earlier focus, and in Massage class, very basic things such as body mechanics, noticing energy, our own as well as others and the five basic massage strokes: effleurage, petrissage, kneading, tapotement and friction. Eventually, Anatomy came into play and both classes were in alignment with each other with Massage class reiterating with the physical body what we had learned in A&P. The rest of the class time was filled with Polarity Therapy, Ortho-Bionomy™ and Jin Shin Do. All of this touching was bound to open up, well, anything really. Tears sometimes, laughter or fear, I even got a migraine once, which gave me absolute empathy and compassion to migraine sufferers; they are nothing like a headache, for those that don't understand.

My main reason for going to massage school was to "heal the healer". I knew my picking up of and carrying my clients physical pain was not preferable and I realized I had much to learn about myself. I had no idea how my experiences at this school would provide deep support for my own healing. This next story is an example:

Jin Shin Do is a form of bodywork based on Chinese Acupuncture, Japanese Jin Shin Jitsu, Taoist Philosophy and western psychology. Using finger-point pressure with strong hands, one holds acupressure points to facilitate an opening between the points. Receiving this Body-Mind Acupressure is exceedingly relaxing and I still love to give and receive this work with my friends and family! When I was still doing bodywork as my living and profession, I would pull JSD out of my quite extensive toolbox when nothing else seemed to work for a particular client. Everyone in class was either on a table receiving or standing/sitting as they gave the treatment. I will say that what follows has never happened in my years as a bodyworker, and JSD sessions are normally exquisite.

One day my instructor was working on me. I had a vision come into my head and simultaneously burst into grief-stricken sobs. She calmly asked me what was happening and I told her the vision. I was standing in a circle of women on a cliffside with the ocean nearby. I was 14. We were all wearing white and we were in sacred ceremony. There was a beautiful white stallion in the middle of our circle and the full moon caused the magnificent animal to glow. Suddenly a tall man strode into the center of our circle and cut the throat of the stallion, black blood pouring. I stopped the memory in shock and my instructor gently helped me calm my breath and come back to the present.

I knew that was a past life and the memory stayed with and disturbed me for years. It wasn't until I met my boyfriend seven years later that the rest of the story came to me. Remember the boyfriend that had St. Vitas' Dance as a child? Well, he and I shared not only this lifetime but that lifetime together, and the rest of the pieces to this puzzle were revealed to me, several months into that relationship. I shall reveal the full puzzle to YOU a few years down the road in the storytelling.

Another "other-worldly" thing that happened to me in massage school happened one morning during the required 8am meditation class. The interesting thing about these classes is that there was a large variety of meditation opportunities. A First Nations/Native American led us in meditation one day. We had Zen Buddhist exposure and another facilitator with an Hindu influence. This could look a variety of ways. Sometimes we would sound, possibly with an ohm, or with a gong, sometimes we would sit in silence. Sometimes we would have a guided meditation inviting us to go to our "happy place", meaning a stream in the woods, sitting atop a mountain in the sun, laying on the beach listening to ocean waves or whatever nature-inspired happy place we had. There was no strict guidance here; it was more of an exploration into relaxation and then listening to what our inner voice or Deepest Soul Selves would suggest. Meditation was very new to most of us and all of the students came from very different walks of life. So this class was like a Meditation 101 class.

One morning, with a similar invitation of a relaxation/happy place, I found I was in a very large spaceship above the earth. It was a busy place, filled with different looking beings. There were a few humans there but mainly beings that didn't look human. I was met by one of the non-humans who greeted me in a gentle but no-nonsense manner, and gave me a short tour. I had little time and what I now recall is there was a very large screen in which I could see some of the Earth. I seemed to be in a "control" room, and most of the people in the room were working in endeavors related to Earth. I felt no malice from anyone, and just a casual interest from some as if an Earthly visitor happened often. I felt I was in my astral body. It seemed only minutes when I heard the facilitator call us back from our meditation. I reluctantly left my spacial guesthouse.

When I opened my eyes I was in the meditation circle and, to be honest, a little disappointed. I was thrilled about my adventure and kept that experience to myself until the evening when I called Mom. Mom's interests had expanded over the years and when I told her what happened she said to me "that is the Ashtar Command Ship". Well, I didn't know what that was but have heard the term many times since. What was known then and is known now has evolved. At the time, the first entry of the knowledge of Ashtar Command into the general public was in 1952 when a channeler, George Van Tassel, was contacted by them. They said they were there to keep the world from a nuclear event. One can research this and more, but it was a little titillating for me at the time. Of course there was no Google or even internet then, so my busy school life continued nonplussed, taking each day at a time, always curious as to what other wonders were in store for me.

I learned many more things about myself, my body and it's energy fields, and emotions that I regularly suppressed. We were in a cocooned environment so to speak, and it was an immersion into a healing paradigm. In addition to regular circles of safe, supportive interactions and calm peaceful communications, the break room was caffeine and sugar free. That was tough. The intention was to bring our attention to those addictions and what we used them for. Some students took that challenge on in a full way, although for me, outside of school was another matter regarding sugar, caffeine and alcohol. Even so, I felt safe in the school and free to be in my exploration of my deeper psyche and emotional realms, albeit with plenty of bumps along the road.

I have had a migraine three times in my life. Several years before, I flew back to Tennessee and met up with my Mom and Aunt Willa and their brother, my Uncle Johnny, for my Grandmother's funeral, with Elise coming up as well from Georgia. We traveled together in a car to my birth land and the three siblings homeland, the Great Smokies near Sevierville (yes, the home of Dolly Parton) and close to Gatlinburg. In the South, taking photos of the body in the casket was a normal occurrence but I was shocked when I saw it. I met my great-great auntie who looked exactly like my beloved great grandma. I was in the heart of my southern family and the grief was thick in the air. Wailing would have been the perfect course, but "dignity" prevailed. I loved being with my family, but I now understand that the grief my family tightly reined in affected my empathic nature in a huge way. After the funeral, we women stopped at a retreat center in Georgia on the way to taking Terese home. I had my first migraine there. It was a shocked agony I never had experienced or certainly understood. The suppressed emotions, mine and others, won the day.

The second migraine was a total shock to me! The school had an interesting policy of six weeks of intensive study and one week off. The "off" for me was driving to Roswell, staying at my parents house and seeing as many massage clients as I could. One would think I'd be happy to be off from my studies for a week but I dreaded the break the first time it came. I was in absolute awe of the wee openings of knowledge, awareness and sensitivity in which I was finding myself immersed and I desperately wanted to keep those tender ways. Going home to my parent's house, as much as I loved them, would put me back into the heavy domain of dysfunction, anger, regret; two people operating on top of deep grief attempting to tolerate their lives. I was afraid I would lose whatever I had gained in my life in Santa Fe.

It was the last day of our classes before our first break and the pain whelmed up and put me down. Luckily, we were in one of our bodywork classes and I just lay on a table in agony, unable to participate. One of my classmates offered to work on me and I had my first Reiki experience. I gratefully felt much better; the pain level diminished significantly although I was thickheaded at the end of class when I was moving about. You migraine sufferers may be shocked at the quick results of my forty minute Reiki session, but the pain was nearly gone! One of my instructors, recognizing what I did not as to the reason I got the migraine, coached me in putting whatever my worries were in a box on a shelf and letting them rest there until I was ready to come back and look at them. That also helped me negotiate the migraine. I went home the next day and was happy to be there with people who I loved and who loved me.

The third and last migraine of my life came on me with one of my long weekend excursions: Friday to Roswell, work, Sunday to Socorro, see the husband but got waylaid and didn't make it back to school until Tuesday. I awakened early Monday, again in deep agony. Drawing out the actual divorce was telling on me and all the unsaid things weighed on my heart and in my head; nearly 10 years of unsaid things, actually. Those that know me now know I have learned to be brave and bold in sharing my heart and that lack of communication is not my foible any more.

I learned to be a deep listener in school; to both another's energy field and to mine. This was just the beginning of allowing myself to sense into things freely, similar to what I did in nature as a wee girl. When doing this with clients, I had also learned some basic tools of how to take care of my self through proper body mechanics and my breath, creating an intentional protective energetic field around me with my mind and allowing only energies of the highest unconditional love to enter my field. This took practice and time was what I had.

Even though I was actually shut down to the concept of "helpers" then, I accepted a known, general Universal Love. However, I was intentionally closed to any guides, angels, entities, even my ancestor helpers that had passed. This was a period of my life where I was throwing off the oppressive yolk of the male dominated Catholic religion and the patriarchal version of a male god. In doing this, I moved to the opposite end of the spectrum and explored the concept of the Divine Feminine and my own internal strength. I studied female archetypes and goddesses of various religions, but interestingly looked to no one but myself, to make my spiritual way in the world. This does not mean I had no Guides, Angels or Ancestors assisting me along the way. As with all of us, just because we don't acknowledge or feel our helpers doesn't mean they are not there. It is my learning that there is even more assistance available when we are willing participants in our spiritual evolution. I was firmly certain, however, I was exactly where I needed to be.

CHAPTER 15
The Roswell Incident

One last "other-worldly" event occurred while I was in massage school in 1989, but before I speak of it, I'd like to give you a little background.

When I was in high school, outside of Columbus, Ohio, my first love was Georgie, a very tall, happy-go-lucky young man. With my Dad's urging, in 1975 Georgie joined the Air National Guard right out of high school and went to Lackland Air Force Base in Texas for eight weeks of Basic Training. I do not remember if it was before he left or after he returned that his best buddy's Dad shared a story with his son and Georgie. This story was top secret but as many people involved in the Incident have done since, the burden was too great to carry and they leaked it to the public. There was a little alcohol to "grease the wheels" so to speak. Georgie then later relayed to me what he had been told.

When Word War II ended in 1945, his buddy's Dad worked at what was then called Wilbur Wright Air Field outside of Dayton, Ohio. Later in 1952, it was renamed and is now known as Wright Patterson Air Force Base or Wright Pat. He was a member of the Military Police with the highest level security clearance. I do not know how long he was there but he was assigned security at a special location on the base during this story, which is set in 1947. I only remember these few details about the telling. Very high ranking military officials, several civilians and medical staff passed through the doors that he guarded. Once he was afforded a glance and he saw something that haunted him for the rest of his life: an alien that was small in stature with a big head. This is the only thing I can remember now. I don't remember if he said it was alive, dead, standing or on a table. I was not surprised at the time when Georgie relayed the story because I always suspected we weren't the only ones in this universe. Having visited Roswell a few times with my family I thought it was interesting and never doubted the truth of the story. For a trusted Military Police Officer to say anything nearly 30 years later, a man who had seen action during World War II, this huge breach of protocol must have weighed heavily on him. I filed this away and a few years down the road I moved to Roswell.

We shall skip ahead of the massage school event in order to share another story, which may give more context to the Santa Fe adventure.

Once again, a mention of my gifted boyfriend: in 1997 which was the 50th Anniversary of the Roswell Incident, he and I were visiting with his dad one day and he told us this story. In 1947, Mr. B was working at the cotton gin in town on the midnight shift. As he always did at the end of his shift, he walked over to the coffee shop on Main Street to have coffee with a few friends before going home. While there, they saw a crowd gathering and they went outside. Coming down the middle of Main Street traveling south was an Army convoy moving very slowly. He saw an enormous object on a flatbed trailer mostly covered by several army tarps, although the edges were somewhat exposed. It was so big that the widest sections of the saucer were nearly scraping the light polls on either side of the street. "Flying Saucer" was being whispered while the crowd solemnly watched the procession. I do not remember if Mr. B said he knew of the newspaper articles the morning he observed this strange parade. The first story of the discovery of a saucer had been published a day or two prior to the full recovery and transport of the craft.

World War II ended September 2, 1945 and the country was still reeling and recovering in July, 1947. The USA was preparing to head into another war, The Korean

Conflict. Roswell was highly familiar with military operations because 1941 saw the Roswell Army Air Field being built. It was heavily used during the war and in 1946 the name was changed to Walker Air Force Base and became the largest Strategic Air Command base in the world. We still have missile silos all around the countryside, albeit empty of missiles (here's hoping). Being a patriotic bunch, when your Government tells you that what they in fact said was a UFO was not a UFO, but a weather balloon, then by golly the citizenry said, "Weather balloon it is!" To this day, there is much undercurrent of this event in the subsequent generations.

Now, back in Santa Fe in 1989, my housemate saw an ad placed in the newspaper by the Santa Fe Public Library stating there was a free event by a channeler on UFOs. We decided to go. I do not remember the gentleman's name, but he was a nice man and introduced himself to us with a disclaimer of sorts. He explained his Guides had been bugging him for years now to offer readings about UFOs and he refused. He shared he had had a UFO experience as a boy with his Mother when they were driving somewhere. He also said he'd resisted UFO readings because he was already considered weird enough in that he channeled, but he finally agreed.

In defense of channels in general: channels do not set out looking for someone/entities to channel. These gifted people do not wake up one day saying, "Gee, I think I'll upend my whole life and start listening to a disembodied voice and tell people all about it." When a person channels, it is because they have decided/agreed to put their previously personal lives on the backburner in order to help individuals and the world at large in a very unique way.

Five of us had gathered to hear what this gentleman and his guides had to say to the public for the first time. There was a man who sat beside me and two women who I believe were friends. My understanding is that my housemate and I were the new ones to the group and the others knew the channel from either previous sessions and/or friendships.

We quieted and he took about the same amount of time as the first channel I'd seen months before, and then began speaking. His voice was less emotional, not as lyrical as the other channeled beings, and they spoke a similar blessing and statement of well-wishes and gratitude for being there to assist. What progressed for the next 35 minutes or so was his channels' speaking highlights about us as individuals and then taking questions.

I don't remember the order of the spoken points as it was 34 years ago. They greeted the man next to me, welcomed him back and appreciated his mind and brilliant insights and rational thinking. He told me he was an engineer at Los Alamos Labs. They spoke to me, saying I have the vibrations of the Great Crystal about me, having lived a life on Atlantis working with the great crystal. I was told I can easily use crystals in my healing work and should do so. I was also one of the ones that knew and worked with the Pleiadians when they arrived on Earth. I was fascinated with their pink skin and the fact they mated in family units of six. They also said that I had Pleiadian lineage [sic] because I had been on one of the first ships that traveled to Earth, since the technology of the time took much longer for travel, and many of us had spent time in cryosleep, as we now call it.

I do not remember if they spoke to my roommate, but addressed one of the other women, stating that she and I had shared a lifetime in Ireland centuries before. I then had an image of us women in a circle in sacred ceremony, said something to that effect, and she confirmed she saw the same thing. I knew it was the lifetime I had seen in Jin Shin Do class.

They eventually opened up for questions. My neighbor, the engineer, asked a question about ship propulsion technology which I cannot now remember. The answer was as incomprehensible as the question, but I admired this man's ability to stay effectively in the conversation. They spoke back and forth for a bit on the subject. I then asked, being from Roswell, if The Roswell Incident actually happened. The question opened up the topic for the rest of the session. There were many things said, but I relay only what I can remember. I do not want to possibly fabricate anything because there is so much sensationalism around this topic.

"Yes" was the answer. The UFO actually crashed between Roswell and Corona, New Mexico. Another crash occurred near Clovis/Portales during the same period of time. The Roswell crash occurred because the ship was flown by young beings that hadn't been to Earth before. It was standard to fly the ships with their minds and when they entered Earth's atmosphere they were overwhelmed with the fear and hate they encountered and they lost control. There were four beings on the ship (although there are many popular reports of only three) and two were killed on impact. One was well and another was injured but alive. Later, the injured one was intentionally allowed to die as part of an experiment involving it's breath and nitrogen content. I don't remember if the "spacemen" needed more or less, but the ones in charge had received the communication of the injured's needs from the uninjured one. I remember feeling deeply sad when I heard the one had, in essence, been murdered. The beings and spacecraft and crash materials were moved to another location, and since the accident the government has been working with extraterrestrials.

The questions and discussions touched on crop circles, abductions and the truths, fallacies and science behind that.

It was an intense experience and my waking and sleeping hours were inundated with the information for a while. Of course, I called Mom again to share my experience.

Rather soon, however, the adventure was left behind as my learning continued in massage school and I needed to be as present as possible to journey the ways of bodywork, schoolwork, energy, emotions, friends, family and the Life in front of me!

I graduated from The New Mexico Academy of Advance Healing Arts May of 1990, continued to live in that beautiful, sacred place for another year or two, developing my skills and private practice as well as working at resorts and health clubs. There was a saying in Santa Fe at the time "there is a massage therapist under every Chamisa bush" because of the two fabulous international schools there and the reluctance of graduates to move back to wherever "home" was. Even so, I always had enough work and faithful clients in Santa Fe, and I still saw clients when I visited Mom and Dad in Roswell.

There was a popular bumper sticker at the time I loved that made me laugh: "Welcome to Santa Fe. Now go home." Well I did just that! I moved to Lincoln, New Mexico, (historical Billy the Kid and Lincoln County Wars location) in 1991 for a short stint and then back home to Roswell in 1992.

This next phase of my life might be considered the most evolutionary aspect to date. I was finally taking all of the advice I've given to you so far in this book as this is the period I learned…well, me. So take heart; "me", and "we" come to find out, are pretty wonderful beings, with all our glorious fabrics brilliantly colorful, ripped and torn, repaired and enduring and we have plenty to love and appreciate!

CHAPTER 16
Freedom is a Fine Thing

I felt all of my life experiences had pointed me in this new direction, which is always true, of course, but this was a significant time of my active, intentional learning more about myself, my gifts, my energies, other's energies through my work with additional classes on Cranial Sacral Therapy, Shock and Trauma Resolution, Polarity Therapy and Ortho-Bionomy™. My active participation in Re-Evaluation Counseling which began in Santa Fe, allowed me to dive into my history, patterns, traumas, failures and celebrations. All of this was hugely freeing to me. I lived life during this period of intense curiosity as to what was happening now, in the current moment and what was around the corner. I honestly don't know if I have felt this mental freedom since and now that I am writing this, I am going to take this segment of "feeling perfect freedom" and explore how I can integrate that in a deeper way into my current life!

An example of this curiosity: I would sit at a client's feet and allow their ankles to rest in my hands as I listened very deeply to their Cranial Sacral Pulse. While being in these alpha and theta brain waves' state, in addition to finding their CS pulse, I may become aware of an entity in the room, maybe two. In order to do these "deeper listening" or immersion therapies, I opened my awareness the best I could, and I can say now it was a similar feeling to raising my antenna. As time went on, I listened and understood usually the entity was their angel or guide, or maybe an ancestor or occasionally a guide, angel or ancestor of mine. I would feel or know that they were there to advocate more healing of the person on the table. Many times the client would say "it feels like your hands are still on my knees" after they realize I had moved somewhere else and it was my best sense that it was not me or me alone.

This may be a similar journey others have in massage therapy or another healing modality training, especially these days, as energy is known and explored in a much bigger way than 35 years ago. My explorations of these things continued throughout my years of bodywork and continue still to this day.

There are two distinctions I wish to make: Even with all the deep listening I was doing and learning during these early massage years, I still didn't recall my very early years of working with my veil or antenna. It isn't until writing my story and the very deep dives into my memories around the trauma and abuse of my childhood I have done in order to write honestly, that I realized I used my antenna at a very early age as I described earlier in the book. Although I am certain I shut down that exploration tool by the age of nine when I could stand no more external input for survival's sake, I have been using it intentionally and actively for 30 or so years now. My re-membering of my veil has been a gradual process throughout the years.

The second distinction I wish to make is that interestingly enough, all this "touchy feely" stuff I had been experiencing since massage school, didn't immediately make it's way into the fully embodied sensate part of my being. Meaning, I realized/learned in school I had been living not fully in my physical body; my etheric self was a little off to the side of my body. This happens to most of us who have experienced deep trauma. That can feel many different ways. For instance, a therapist would place their hands on both legs, feet and knees, and I would feel one side much more than the other. This happened all the way up my body. Sometimes it felt like one side of me was wrapped in cotton. During those days, it was almost always the left side of my body, considered by some to be the feminine side, the receiving, emotional side. It was a many year process of receiving bodywork, earthing as we now call it, balanced physical activities like bellydance and Tai Chi and various movement therapy explorations such as Continuum and Continuum Movement that brought me fully into my body. I occasionally have a temporary feeling of not being fully embodied but there are many things I do to explore and rectify that, including the above mentioned. This disconnection within myself led me into an 11 year love/hate relationship with my new best/worst friend.

CHAPTER 17
Fear is my Friend

Anxiety attacks suck. If you don't personally know, just ask anyone who has had one. I was the last person in the world who I thought would have an anxiety attack. I knew all about (or so I thought) how to get calm, breathe well, relax, live that massage therapy-ish lifestyle, but that dragon still burned my butt.

I would get up every morning and go down to a local donut shop close to my place, buy a newspaper and a cake donut, do the crossword puzzle, drink coffee, eat my donut and smoke a few cigarettes. I deeply enjoyed this ritual I had made for myself and every weekday began like this.

One morning, mid-drag, I began feeling quite weird. I felt this strange, big sensation in my low back area that gave me huge tingles as it started moving up my spine. It was an all-encompassing feeling and as it traveled up intense fear arose with it. I had to move! I grabbed my keys and left, freaking out as I made my way to my car. Whatever this feeling was kept growing and my breath started coming in shallow waves as I could feel my chest constrict. I got home quickly and called my Aunt Willa who came immediately. It seemed like forever before she got there as my panic was in full force: heart pounding, cold sweat, brain and body in full fight or flight mode but I wasn't thinking rationally enough to even figure that out.

When she walked in the door I don't remember exactly what she said or what happened, but I learned later she understood what was happening. I know she talked to me, likely had me breathing with some control and I know her presence made me feel slightly safer. The hardest part was not knowing what was happening. I had heard of panic or anxiety attacks but didn't recognize that I was having one.

I was eventually able to talk which helped me get some of the internal pressure out. If I could have had a good cry that would have helped immensely, but flight or fight response doesn't have time to stop for those niceties.

I eventually called my friend Joy, who was also a Re-Evaluation Co-counselor, and that afternoon I had an RC session which was very helpful in terms of getting even more of the pressure out. RC requires we be both a client (I had lots of tears and shaking, all great releases) and then when we are done being a client, we shift to being a counselor which requires us to be in rational thinking mode. I had good training in that and was out of any active physical panic symptoms by the end of our session, however, I was exhausted and felt wrung out.

This all sounds easy-peasy, right? Everything is fine and dandy now? Wrong. I never had a full-blown panic attack again. But what was I left with? Well, it took me a couple of weeks before I could go to the grocery store, or anywhere really. I didn't want to leave my house at all. When I worked up the courage to do so, someone went with me and I was in a fairly elevated anxiety state for the duration. I overcame the inability to do things and go places by myself eventually. Prior to the attack, I had been a lone wolf most of my life. I LIKED going places alone most times because I enjoyed my own company. I did ALOT of work around this issue: co-counseling (which also included physical activity co-counseling), and I studied the known facts around panic attacks because for me, when I understand something, things are more manageable. I did things to lower my stress hormone levels like drink less coffee, get more sleep, afore mentioned RC, dance, take loads of Rescue Remedy, a Bach Flower Remedy for stress, trauma and anxiety (I've carried a small bottle with me for years for myself and others including animals), drink relaxing herbal teas and I remembered that sex is a great stress reliever!

This is what I discovered: from that day forward, the FEAR of the event happening again was the actual cause of symptoms arising, and arise they did! I also discovered I was more afraid of the event coming on in public instead of when I was alone because I would be alone within that experience. An interesting conundrum, yes? I tracked the source of that fear down in co-counseling sessions and found it to be a crib-based feeling from my parents arguing fiercely in another room. I was terrified of the anger and alone in that terror because my safety people were not safe. Thus, I developed a pattern of feeling safer alone than with others. At this time in my life, I prefer solitude the majority of the time, but I am never alone.

Even when I realized several months later the cause of the attack, it was 11 years before I had a reliable handle on the physical flight or fight response. So, "I never had a full blown attack again" means I never had the complete meltdown again, but I had years of fear that heightened incrementally and physical symptoms that grew with/because of the fear. Many of you know the sensations that arise. I had plenty of hair raising scalp prickles which led to every hair on my body standing up and I would be off and hopefully "not running". I would go into action doing the things I had learned that would diminish or at least calm the symptoms. As time went on, the symptoms arose less and less.

There are many things I have learned having had the opportunity to experience this first hand. I discovered the panic attack started when I had my first and only full on Kundalini experience. It was the weirdest, totally unbeknownst energy feeling I have ever had. I didn't REALIZE what it was and it triggered terror in my body. Apologies to any Kundalini therapists out there but this is what it was for me. Had I had any learning in the matter previously, it would have been a wild and interesting ride, but likely not terrifying. I have had loads of energetic experiences within and without my body since then, along with feeling Kundalini movement, but that opening was like a tidal flood of energy that I certainly didn't appreciate for what it was. I also suspect my buried childhood trauma was the source of the terror. Even though I had been working on it for a few years "mentally" so to speak, in talk therapy and co-counseling, there was still pa-lenty of buried physical sensations of the trauma that I am certain were released in the huge energy flow originating in my coccygeal area, which then triggered and carried the terror. The imbalance of the root and sacral chakras can relate to many things including insecurity, fear, feeling disconnected to Earth, creativity and/or sexual issues.

A most wonderful learning from this experience is that I was eventually drawn into Shock and Trauma Resolution Therapy. "Healer heal thyself," right? My school offered many additional programs and I was thrilled to start learning in this field. *Waking the Tiger* by Peter Levine with Ann Frederick published in 1997, began my official journey of my personal work and Body/Somatic Therapy I offered to clients. I called my work "Injury Resolution" instead of "Shock and Trauma Resolution" because those words alone can be pretty "heightening" for someone dealing with anxiety and Panic Disorder caused by traumatic event(s). The book and work was revolutionary at the time and it opened the field of Somatic Therapy. Today there are loads of offerings in mind/body trauma healing.

Part and parcel of healing trauma-causing anxiety for me was to practice what Buddhism offers which is the observing mind. What this meant for me was to not get "mentally or emotionally attached" to sensations in my body that felt like panic. I would mentally take a step back and observe what my body was doing by being curious and not judging or attaching emotions to the sensations. I would take whatever steps I felt necessary to help these symptoms but wouldn't allow my mind or emotions to get on the panic train. I also learned that in the physical body, excitement and fear is the same physiological response. This "observing mind" practice gets easier and easier as time goes on as practice makes perfect, right?

I flew into New York City on an American Airlines flight on September 18, 2001 and there were no passengers besides me and my friend. I was several years into my healing and handling of rising anxiety, and I loved the empty flight, although I felt much compassion towards the flight crew. It was my sensitivity to others' energy and their mental/emotional state that caused my anxiety to be waiting in the sidelines for possible triggering. But herein lies the knowing; my projected fear of the future, of something that HAD NOT EVEN HAPPENED, was my doppelgänger.

Panic Disorder can be debilitating. This is my story of how I dealt and still occasionally deal with the aftereffects of ONE single, full-out Panic Attack I had over thirty years ago. I know people who have PD have their own methods of coping in order to manage their life. It is my prayer that my story can give a little ease and possibly hope for these people, as well as possibly a better understanding for the rest of us who don't understand this phenomena.

If there is anything one can learn from this chapter share, it is that "being in the present" IS the most powerful way to live in the world. We hear that all the time, but it is so very true. I certainly don't have the perfect handle on it, and that's ok. What do I do to become present? The best and easiest way is to Earth. I am sitting here with my geranium plant which needs cutting back and some fertilizer. I will breathe now, focusing only on my breath (well, and the keyboard, but you get my drift). I already feel more grounded even with the typing and I notice the beautiful veins in the leaves. I am still, for a few moments. Shortly I'm going outside, to lift my face to the sun, take my shoes and socks off and sit with my feet on the ground. Being grateful. Breathing. Loving.

CHAPTER 18
The Thing Called Death

My first willing participation in a death experience was with my sister and her beloved doberman, Francis. All her dogs had names derived from her favorite saint, St. Francis of Assisi, Patron Saint of Animals. Francis was a red doberman, a floppy-eared sweetheart who had sinus cancer and was on her last 48 hours or so. Elise knew she would soon make the decision to have our wonderful vet come out to her house to release Francis from her body.

I was living in Santa Fe and told my various employers at the spas and resort my niece was dying and I was going home to Roswell to be with my family. All true statements! When I arrived at the house, Francis was still conscious, drinking a little water and she may have gotten up with help once or twice to pee. It would be the next day when we released her. Meanwhile, true to my spiritually invested family, Francis was decked out! My Aunt Willa had a castor oil pack on the top of her head (a la Edgar Cayce), we had tall, religious Christian candles lit around the room, some East Indian incense burning, Sai Baba vibhuti spread all over her head and cheeks and various songs playing on the cassette player including East Indian chants, Benedictine Monks and Hildegard Von Bingen Gregorian chants. But the most impressive thing was that we had taped a crystal to each one of Francis' chakras. We had amethyst, clear quartz, lapis lazuli, carnelian and others, but the coup de gras was a beautiful large emerald ring of my aunts' taped to her heart area.

When the vet stopped by that evening to have a look at her, he came into the room, looked around, and unfazed because he knew our family, quietly asked for us to turn on some more lights so he could see. After he examined her he agreed tomorrow was the day.

The next day he arrived. Elise and I sat with Franny and all was calm and beautiful. When he was finished, he quietly left, telling me to make sure we folded her legs up tightly as if she was sleeping because she was big dog and the grave would be a considerable dig. I sat back down and kept my hands on her with every sense I had alert to any changes within her body. I could feel after two quiet minutes or so, a thick warmth begin to emanate from her body and my felt sense was it was her astral body. That energetic feeling dissipated in about four minutes. In about five minutes after the injection, I felt/saw a huge energy fill the room and heard her barking, and then saw in my mind's eye Francis hunkered down wagging her little stub ready to P L A Y!!! I relayed this to Elise and she continued talking to her, as she had been throughout, telling her it was great for her to go play, go have fun, she loved her very much and to please come back to visit as much as she wanted. Elise was very sensitive and told me weeks later Franny came pretty regularly for a while. She could often feel her jump on the bed at bedtime for a few weeks after she left her body.

We had a funeral for her the next day, photographs displayed, stories told; we sang, dug a pretty darned big hole and planted a rose bush on top of her. The several of us who had gathered to bury her and celebrate her shared a meal that evening. During the meal Aunt Willa remembered her emerald ring was still taped to Francis, buried under the rose bush. Lots of laughter ensued! Elise offered to find somebody to dig Francis and the ring up, but Auntie decided to leave it with Francis. If people in the future ever dig up my family's animal graves that are spread around New Mexico, they certainly will know how beloved our fur companions were!

My next death experience was shortly after with my own Doberman. Portia had gone down in her rear end and I took her to an excellent vet in Albuquerque who discovered a blockage in her lumbar vertebrae. In the x-rays it was difficult to see if her symptoms were connected to a disc that was herniated or possibly a tumor encompassing the disc and vertebrae. She performed a Myelogram, which is injecting ink into the cerebral spinal fluid and taking X-rays. The procedure was very long because she couldn't get the dye to move past the blockage and Portia was under a long time. I brought her home still unable to walk, without answers. We agreed to take a few breaths before deciding the next steps.

Portia's pain was severe as she came fully out of the anesthesia. She was in anguish, and aspirin didn't touch it. (I use CBD these days if necessary, but only with the knowledge of my vet.) I was up with her nearly all night, and at one point, she simply stopped breathing. I started CPR on her and when her hackles rose, I immediately stopped. I didn't expect her to go, but it was time. I did the same as I did with Francis, leaving my loving hands on her, calmly telling her it was okay, she was a good dog and I loved her. I felt the exact same feeling as I did with Franny. After a minute or two I could feel a thick warm energy sensation emanate out of her body and then the feeling stopped. I assumed her astral body left her physical body.

I tried hard to see, hear or feel her like I did with Franny, but I was honestly in shock. I wasn't prepared for her to go. I had vague senses of her, but not the happy dog vision which would have been very comforting. I missed her. I grieved her. I felt a deep emptiness. Interestingly, nearly 4 weeks later my divorce papers finally came in the mail, and they were signed the exact same day Portia died. She was given to us by strangers shortly after Jacky had been nearly killed in the motorcycle accident very early in our marriage.

She was there for most of our marriage and left when it was over. She saw me through.

My next direct experience with death was nearly two years later, helping a dear friend of the family who finally succumbed to cancer. Darlene was in hospital with my Mother attending her and two other loving friends and I there for support. Her time to leave was near. We had all been at her bedside and everyone but Mom left for a few minutes. I went back in from the hallway, and Darlene had stopped breathing maybe two minutes before. Mom, grief-stricken and in shock, was being "busy" with neatening things. I immediately went to Darlene's side because I was learning I was a good presence to hold space for beings leaving their body and, selfishly so, I was also very curious about the process of deathing. My other friend came in to quietly be with my Mother, who loved Darlene deeply. Maybe five minutes into my arrival back into the room, I "saw" and reported to Mom and our friend, that I had just seen Darlene come through the wall with Portia beside her! She had her hand on top of Portia's head as she would do when they were both alive. I was surprised as I had forgotten they loved each other very much and it had been nearly two years since Portia had died! I then saw Darlene jump up, kick her heels together and exclaim "wahoo!!" again confirming for me (as I sometimes need, when I doubt my senses) I wasn't making things up. I never even had SAID the word "wahoo" before I relayed it to Mom and our friend.

Today, when I reflect upon this, even though Portia and Darlene loved each other very much and Portia, naturally, was one of the many spiritual beings there to assist her in her crossing over, I also feel Spirit assisted in their coming together into the room as a learning for me to trust myself and my senses even more.

I have had many deathing and passed soul experiences since those times, but I wish to share two more significant ones. Mom and Dad divorced several years before Mom passed away in 2003. Several months before mom passed, Dad had a stroke. Even so, he stayed mobile and always busy with his ham radio and radio club, computers, church and other social activities. At 83, he still made regular trips to visit his lady friend about an hour away. In his last years, I regularly heard him say after my rolling eyes would follow his overt stare at a beautiful woman, "I'm OLD I'm not DEAD!"

The challenge from his stroke was in his brain pathways related to speech. By then, research had shown that brain activity begins imitating the person or people with whom one is gathered. (Science-based reason to choose one's companions wisely. And stay away from those mobs! They truly became a mass mind.) Dad and I found that to be true as I began my daily interactions with him to help with any communication or medical needs he had. It was amazing when we were together and having a conversation, because my own words became harder to find. Since he was a chatty person, a stroke didn't stop him from communicating however he could. The results of these conversations nearly always ended in gales of laughter.

The upshot of these times with Dad is that I fell in love with him a few short years before his death. During that time, I learned more about his life and his experiences and his feelings about his relationships than I did in our whole life previously. I became grateful for his stroke because it softened him and I truly saw into the man he was. As close as I was with my Mom during our lifetime together, it is my Dad for whom my heart weeps the most. And even though I can see and hear my passed family, the heart wants what the heart wants, as they say, and I grieve his loss more.

One day I got a call from his lady friend that he had not shown up the night before as he usually did on a weekend. I feared the worst because he always communicated, by phone or ham radio (she was a ham also). I walked into his living room and found him sitting in his chair in front of a beautiful picture on his computer screen which he loved and reminded him of heaven. He knew he was dying and brought the picture up as he moved into his death process. I saw him slumped there and I said out loud "Oh, Dad!" and started crying "crocodile tears" as he called them. Immediately after I started crying, I became aware of his presence in the corner of the room and heard him gruffly say in my mind, "Oh I'm all right!" and I said out loud to him, "I know YOU are, it's me I'm crying for." I could feel his surprise that I heard him. I am sure he probably realized then that the women in his life, Mom, Aunt Willa, Elise and I may have been right about many things we had tried to share with him. It was a pleasure, I must say, hearing him speak normally even if it was between minds.

As souls do, Dad would drop in to observe funeral arrangements in between whatever else he may have been up to in his brand new, shiny wings. I didn't know he was visiting me one day when I was busy working on the computer choosing the songs for his mass. I picked songs I knew he loved, and for the Recessional, when we leave with the casket, I chose an old song by The Impressions, "Amen", a military sounding Gospel song. I was mentally involved doing the song transfer and was interrupted by Dad saying "You're ALL RIGHT!" a phrase he would say occasionally as his highest praise, being a man not taken to verbal niceties. It was great to know he approved.

Dad had quite a sendoff; a funeral mass, memorial party afterwards, and a military burial the next day amidst a lightening storm in the mountains of Ft. Stanton, New Mexico, in their military cemetery.

The last significant death experience was my Sister's. Elise was living in Kentucky and her death was unexpected and a shock. Since it was an unattended death, an autopsy was ordered. I was told it may be several days before the autopsy was complete and her body could then be released to the crematorium. Since I was the one that needed to handle everything, I took five days or so to take care of business at home because I could be gone for over a month. As I was getting close to leaving time, the very helpful crematorium director who had been in contact with me daily to update me, called to advise me my Sister's body was being released and they would soon be picking her up for the cremation.

I had felt Elise's presence somewhat, having my antenna and veil as available as possible while I was making preparations during those days, but nothing stands out for me now except for this; I was, once again, sitting at my computer working on last minute details, and I heard my Sister's voice, clear as a bell say "BURN baby burn!" Well, heck! I knew what that meant! Elise had said those words occasionally in her years (I never had used that phraseology). Her body had been her painful captive for nearly fifty years and she was de-lighted to leave that body behind! It made me happy hearing those words.

After arriving in Kentucky, I split most of my time between my Aunt and Cousin's house where I slept and made all the necessary phone calls, and my Sister's apartment. I enjoyed being in her apartment alone as I was preparing it for the estate sale. A very entertaining conversation happened in her apartment one afternoon!

Anyone with siblings may have had "borrowing" history as Elise and I did when growing up. I knew she was there and every time I made a decision, I was actively reaching out with my "antenna" for her response. I could feel her tangible pleasure when I took any of her sweet things for mine, although when we were growing up and "borrowing" each other's clothes, the feelings weren't so soft and fuzzy. On this particular day, we got into a bit of an argument and it was truly funny.

I pulled out a beautiful skirt and jacket but it just wasn't my style. I put it in the "for sale" pile and Elise piped up, "No! You take that." Out loud, because many times I talk out loud to Spirit, "No, I don't want it. I don't like it". Elise: "Take it! It'll look good on you." Me: "No! I won't wear it!" Elise again: "Take it!" Me: "I don't want to have to deal with it if I can't wear it!!" Elise: "TAKE IT!" Geez. "Ok" said I, grudgingly. Did I wear it later? A little bit. But it didn't look good on me and I passed it on.

By 2008 I was essentially an orphan with my whole family of origin having died within four years and four months of each other. I also lost my home, my partnership of seven years and seven of my beloved fur companions during that time. Loss was my learning for a while.

I will leave you with this: After death, our loved ones are always available to us when we need or want them. One can learn this now because this is a popular topic accessible via many on-line platforms. Go ahead and talk to them. Every time you talk to them they will hear you. They also evolve and learn after they pass. Your relationship with them wasn't perfect? They now understand and accept their responsibility in that matter. If you could hear them, you might hear them apologize to you. Or not. All is eventually, lovingly resolved when you leave your own body if you wish to have resolution.

The most important thing of all I wish to impart: let go of the guilt. You could not have saved them. All was/is in Divine Order. Do you feel guilty because you weren't there when they passed? It is perfect you were not there. The soul needed you to be gone in order to leave. There was nothing else you could have done to make their life and their death "better". No new drug, no different/better care or treatment, no additional love would have changed the intended course of events. We always do the best we can with the tools we have in any given situation, and remember, each soul has their own path divinely ordered, and their soul must do what it must do. Forgive yourself, for you have done nothing wrong. Let the guilt go and breathe again. Put your feet on the Earth, be thankful for the Life you have right now, in this moment. Breathe and be grateful.

CHAPTER 19
The Chosen One

We are all "The Chosen One". We are all called to use our talents and our gifts to be of service one way or another. It may be service to our family, a neighbor, that very sad customer that just walked into our store. Maybe it is just endeavoring to bring a little light into someone's day. Maybe it is a big mission in life that calls us and we heard that call a long time ago. Or maybe we feel adrift, rudderless with no anchor, as I used to feel after my Mother died.

Those first six years after I graduated from massage school, I had a specific clientele. As I was dealing with my own dragons' fires with migraines, panic and death, most all the clients coming to me had regular migraines, dealt with debilitating anxiety or were either dying themselves or had a family member that was dying. I was fearless. I willingly and regularly looked into the eyes of my dragons, embraced them, and was able to hold space and support a client wherever they were in their healing journey. I'd like to think I may have been able to help and support those clients by giving them encouragement, hope and loving them for exactly who and where they were.

You may have a passion that makes you happy and it can pop up at any age or time of your life. You can be the best "you" while changing the oil in someone's car or stocking the shelves in a grocery store. Your smile, your satisfied energy while doing your job, helps those who benefit from your job because your energy transfers into spaces and things. If you feel you have a calling you haven't been able to put your finger on, or as I said when I was a young adult woman, "I don't know what I want to be when I grow up", that is ok too. You know how to find that nudge in the right direction. It may be a step by step process. Sit by a plant you love, go outside and put your bare feet on the ground, touch a beautiful tree and breathe, be still, be grateful. Your life is right here, right now.

CHAPTER 20
Heartmind: The Free Resource

Once again, remember that little boy early on in this book who also flew? Well, I fell for him when he asked me to dance at a country bar with a huge dance floor I used to go to on the weekends. He was a fine dancer and a strong leader. Be still my beating heart! Life is fickle and serendipitous and if you ask anyone who loves to dance, sometimes that is all it takes! Jacob was my boyfriend for nearly two years, and very early on in our relationship he mentioned a few interesting things about himself and I wasn't fazed. I had friends who were Intuitives, worked with energy and were in the healing arts. Since I also did energy work, he opened up to me as he never had with anyone.

He was raised in a very restrictive family and church when it came to energy work and paranormal experiences. He had been shamed and told it was of the devil so he pretty much kept his gifts to himself until we met, although he had covertly used his gifts for healing or safety purposes for himself or others. Our experiences would take another book but there are a few highlights I'd like to share.

An eye-opening experience happened when we were driving in the mountains not too far from Roswell. It was fall and there were plenty of deer herds crossing the road we were on. I am always concerned about their safety and mentioned it to Jacob. He said, "You don't need to worry about it. Did you see that buck just take that huge leap to get across the road?" I said "Yes!" He said "Well, YOU did that! Your eyes are like lasers and you just shot him a good one in his butt!" He could SEE what happened and I learned from him that we can send energy with our eyes and intention.

If you take a moment, you probably can think of someone you know who has a very piercing glance or look. It is possible they know or maybe don't how they are using their eyes. Play with that concept yourselves, being especially mindful of your angry eyes. Who wants to be on the receiving end of that? I have been playing with it for years now and it feels like very high magic to me. When I am on my motorcycle I use eyes/mind generally. I feel quite Wizard-y. When I am in my car I also use my hand. I will be riding or driving down a road and see a car pulling up to their stop sign, start to pull out and I am not sure if they see me coming! I will use my hand to gesture (not what you think) a wait signal they cannot see because I am in my car, but I use a very strong intention with my eyes, hand and mind. When I am paying attention and do this, I have never had anyone pull out in front of me. I also practice on animals in the road, using my voice, eyes and hands. Like all things, practice makes perfect! Wizard-y.

My boyfriend was in an accident as a young man and broke his back. He was in hospital for a year and the prognosis was he would never walk again. You see, we have three main types of nerves in the body. We have Autonomic Nerves relating to involuntary or partially voluntary functions such as blood pressure, heart rate, digestion and temperature regulation. Next, we have Motor Nerves which move our appendages and basically our whole structure and finally Sensory Nerves which help us feel pressure, heat and pain, as well as see, hear, etc. His motor nerves in his back to his legs were severed.

During his time in the hospital he switched things around. Even though the doctors told him he would be paralyzed for life, he walked away from the hospital after being there for a year. He had the ability to go in to his body, locate the nerves and work on them. He intentionally switched the sensory nerves to become his motor nerves for his legs. When I met him he could not feel his legs from his upper thighs down but was fully mobile, although he had much pain in his back most times. After working with an intuitive friend of mine, he made even more changes to his legs to where he could actually feel them again. It was stunning and deeply moving for both of us when he came out of his session barefoot, to feel the grass under his feet again.

Another interesting thing about his abilities to focus deeply and intently was demonstrated one summer. I had a very favorite coffee cup made by a friend who was no longer with us that I loved, and the handle was broken off. I asked Jacob if he could fix it for me. He said yes, but to stay inside as he needed to go outside barefoot so he could ground well and work for a while. He came in 15-20 minutes later and the handle was attached. He had gone into the structure of the cup down to the molecular level and rebuilt the brokenness. The bottom of the handle was perfect and the top had a wee bump where he had worked. What ability and power we have available to us if we only practice our focus and set our intention!

During this incredibly learning time I had with this man, I finally was able to put all the pieces together for my early BCE Celtic life. I received much of this information during two bodywork sessions, each from trusted friends, which fleshed out the rest of the details.

You will recall the lifetime that came forward during my Jin Shin Do session in massage school where I was part of a group of women in white, standing in a circle by a cliffside with a white stallion in the middle of our circle. A man came into the circle and slit the stallion's neck, black blood flowing in the light of the full moon. I then broke down into sobs. Well, the rest was revealed to me during those bodywork sessions.

My friends were great therapists and during each of the two sessions when I had the memories, I was in a deeply relaxed state of receiving a massage and this is what came to me: I was a young woman of 14 in early Ireland and we women would hold power raising ceremonies to cultivate our religion and culture, to strengthen our village and honor the land. In those early times we aboriginal peoples were deeply connected to the land and our worship, and gratitude entailed circles of song, dance and ritual to strengthen our good fortunes and secure our place in history going forward.

Jacob was sent by the Catholic Church to our land to break the back of the pagan heathens and bring Christianity to the land. He was a priest. He deceptively came as a stranger into our village, humble and kind, bringing gifts. He shyly wooed me and I was swept away by this tall, dark stranger. He gently asked me of what we did, because it was understood we would hand-fast and I would take him to husband, and he wanted to understand to better be a good mate. What we women did was sacred and secret to all, not even our village elders knew what we did. I told him secrets no man should know.

When he strode into the circle he was a huge, menacing evil and I saw enormous horns on his head, although since he was a priest I do not know if he actually was wearing them or if I saw them energetically in that lifetime. I collapsed as the blood fell, as did other women, and some fought him. It was no matter.

When these memories came flooding back, I sobbed even more. I and my vanity were the reason the back of our culture, our religion was broken. My actions and my betrayed heart were the beginning of the downfall of the rich, Celtic Earth-Worshiping religion and the beginning of the oppression of Catholicism.

When I stepped back a bit after these memories arose, I realized that every thing happens as it is supposed to. If it was not me that succumbed, it would have been someone else. I told Jacob when these memories arose and he acknowledged he knew. I do not know if he remembered only as I told him or he had already known when we met. There was not much discussion of this between us. There was no right or wrong, it just was the way it was. It was, however, a huge grief I had carried throughout several lifetimes. I have now had the healing of this event in this lifetime.

It was in 2008 when I spread my Sister's ashes in a magical place in Kentucky called Indian Fort Mountain, east of Berea. Elise and I often went there for music festivals and to hike. It was March, cool, and only sweet small beginnings of Spring were apparent. I sat quietly after hiking up the mountain a ways, calmly preparing for the sacred ceremony of releasing her ashes to the Earth. I opened myself the best I could for this mysteriously significant event in this profound, enchanted place. Then I stood to start dispersing some of her body.

I know now what I did not recognize at the time: I opened my "veil" for the first time in years, decades. My mind and heart was full of gratitude, loss, love of my Sister and what next will be. The ashes were landing, blowing and dancing in the cool spring breeze and I then became aware of a Sprite, a Fairy if you will (although they are slightly different). She was between three and four feet tall, slender and sweetly hiding a bit behind a tree, playing peek-a-boo of sorts. Immediately after seeing her I then saw the circle again, before the blooding. This Sprite had been there on that land, during that time, celebrating and supporting us. And she was there that day in Kentucky, to tell me all was well, all was forgiven. I thanked her and she was soon gone.

I cried tears of relief and no longer carry this burden of lifetimes.

The term, bodymind, has been used for decades, referencing indisputable co-creation of our body's health through the use of the mind. The larger term, "heartmind" is being used now amongst therapists, healers, practitioners, coaches, inspirers and creators, and as I mentioned in Chapter 4, the power of prayer is simply a potent combination of thoughtform, which is mind, and emotion, which is heart; "the two most dynamic and encompassing creators in and of our lives".

Be(a)ware that every thought in your mind is the shaper of your life's events. There is the larger topic of soul co-creation with other souls, but this chapter hopefully inspires you to start trusting your power to create, to inspire, to change things, especially for your Self. This must begin by taking time with nature, to ground. In that process your heart opens and you begin to see and feel beauty. This is the beginning of trusting. You CAN trust your heart. You CAN allow yourself to trust the desire to create something; a different home, peace in your life, a supportive community, a new transportation possibility, a job you love, a lover you love, and on a bigger scale, a life you love!

When you shift you, you shift the world. But YOU first! Baby steps. Feel into your love. Love your love. Love into your desire(s), your passion, think into your desire(s), passion, and become the creator of your life!

CHAPTER 21
Astrally Yours

Because of Jacob's early childhood disease, astral travel became his friend. In our lives together, I was deeply intrigued with the experiences he shared with me and apparently when I was sleeping, I decided to do something about it.

I felt safe with Jacob to explore other worlds that I have, for years, yearned to do. What did that look like? I would wake up in the wee hours of the morning, recalling a fabulous dream and then realizing I felt that there were one or two entities in the room with us and I would be scared. I would say a protective prayer or two and fall back asleep. That happened a few times and then Jacob told me his perspective.

As soon as I was deeply asleep, my astral body would happily traipse off to explore a world or two. (Now my conscious mind would NEVER intentionally do that. I am pretty attached to being in this body of mine.) I would delightedly go somewhere, make friends, let them show me around their place and then I would invite them back to my place to see where I lived! Then I would wake up, sensing a presence or two respectfully off in the corner of the room, and my human physical self would say, "what the fuck!" pray the Our Father like it hasn't been prayed in a while and interestingly, go back to sleep. Meanwhile the friendly other-worldlys would be a bit confused at the lack of welcome. They would then understand MY lack of understanding and go back home to where they came from.

Jacob followed me everywhere. Ya gotta love that. I was safe with that expert making sure I was safe. No wonder my Astral Body was willing to party it up. I remember two planets I visited with two distinct outcomes.

I remember being above a planet that looked like it was covered with a bunch of trees. It kind of reminded me of the dark forest in Wizard of Oz which was scary as a little kid. But it was TREES and I LOVE trees! I curiously went down to investigate. I felt them pulling me in, I mean pulling me down like they would suck me in to ingest me. I was terrified. I fought free of them and zoomed back home to wake up with heart pounding. Aaahh! Geez it was awful! By then, I knew the score about what was happening at night and I cuddled up to my partner and went back to sleep. I told Jacob the next morning and he remembered. He said I was fine. I handled it well and he didn't need to step in. He did, however, know about that planet and that yes, they ate energy and would have loved mine.

The other planet I remember was this amazing place of peace and joy and ease and the people there were like big bubble beings, beautiful and shiny like the bubbles we blow out of a bottle. I don't know how to describe it, especially all these years later, but I still get filled with this sense of joy and delight. They were oh-so-welcoming, and lovingly joyful. And truly, they floated around their planet and were big bubbles. When I shared this with Jacob he said yup, pretty much like that. I am sure there are people who astral travel regularly and may know the planet and can give a more accurate description of it. I do not know if I ever have gone back but I have always wanted to.

The last thing I want to share about the experiences of paranormal I learned from being with this kind, loving but oh-so-very-different man relates a little closer to home. I actually debated as to if I would share this in this book, but I kept hearing "it is important", so here we go!

I had a beautiful friend who was married to a man who was in the United States Air Force. I was so sad when they moved but we kept in touch by letters (those paper things with stamps, return address labels and such) when they were in Italy. I don't remember where her husband was raised, but she grew up in Roswell in the northeast part of town. It is known by many people in town that until the 1960's, a northeast section of town was used as a portal of sorts. My friend, Gloria, remembered growing up in her childhood home, a ranch style house, and waking up in the middle of the night seeing metal equipment being drawn into the walls. She didn't know what was happening and would soon go back to sleep.

Well, shoot forward several years, and she shared her experiences with me and that her husband also had similar experiences. They would both wake up vaguely seeing things disappearing in to their bedroom walls at night and then they would go back to sleep. She knew it was an ET experience and she wanted it to stop. I suggested my fella would be able to provide some insight into the matter. They were living in an Italian town outside an airbase at the time. My honey agreed to help and this is what happened.

We agreed upon a time they would be asleep in Italy for Jacob to begin. I decided to do dishes while he lay down in his recliner to do his thing. This meant he would astral project, leave his body, and go to Italy to talk to the ET's and see what was going on. He had talked with Gloria by phone the day before so he had his own connection to her he could now follow.

He lay down and I began doing the dishes. During my dish cleaning process, I became aware of a tall entity to the left of me. I said something aloud like "Hello. Yes, I am on the other end of this trail." I felt no animosity. Just observation. After about 20 seconds they/it left. Jacob returned/woke up about eight minutes later. This is what I remember of his report and I want to say I am probably not remembering the order in which he gave it.

After he lay down he shortly "left" and went to Gloria and her husband's bedroom where he encountered either them there in a different dimension OR followed the trail to where they all were. (I did not ask specifics at that time.) He learned that her family had been under observation for several generations. When her ancestors arrived in this area it was during her (great-?)grandfather's time. They initially had a farm in the same general area as her family's current house, and the beings followed them, observing and doing tests upon them. The entities were quite surprised when Jacob appeared as they did not know that Gloria and her husband realized they had been visiting them. The upshot of this encounter was that whatever decades long generational experiments had been happening were no longer viable as the results were contaminated. Gloria and her husband's awareness of them polluted the testing ground; they left never to return.

My friend and I spoke on the phone the next day and I relayed what Jacob had told me. She was deeply relieved. She told me her family had also passed down the knowledge that there had always been some UFO/ET activity in the area that was northeast of the city limits. She confirmed a few weeks later the ET experiences had stopped. No more interference of their sleep. I can only imagine the feelings that would come from having this new freedom from this invasive generational paradigm!

CHAPTER 22
Who Let the Dogs Out?

When I met my boyfriend, he had a mama dog who was pregnant and shortly had seven pups, four of which we kept, three for which we found good homes, and three other older pups that eventually found new homes. I brought my two dogs and one cat into the picture and we also acquired two cockatiels with a huge cage. After the dust settled, we lived together for nearly two years with six dogs, a cat and the birds which stayed for a year before rehoming.

With Jacob's encouragement, I learned to listen, hear and communicate fairly well with the animals. He had learned his skills/gifts through trial by fire, so to speak, so he didn't always have a specific way of instructing me; more of a "give it a try and see what happens" school of thought. It is, actually, a good piece of advice.

As with other of my gifts that I allowed to expand when we were together, this one also grew with time and practice. Not only could I listen and hear a dog's thought, sometimes I actually heard a voice. I was shocked when it first happened. Jacob confirmed, yes, they have "thought voices". It was quite funny when I would hear a different timbre or way of "speaking" they had. I would hear a delicate, light voice out of a big dog, or a large, deep voice out of small cat. I couldn't hear everyone's voice, but I would get pictures or feelings of their intention.

I communicated then, and still do now, with words and pictures. Sending and receiving pictures is very workable for animals. I know our dogs, for instances, (cats being of Royalty and leave it to us ignorant humans to figure it out) try in many ways to help us "get it". They are forgiving of our "deaf inner ear", and that's how most of us live with our animals. Love prevails and is most important here.

When I am leaving for a few days, I will sit with my animals and use words and pictures at the same time. The distinctions I use are nighttime supper/bed and I also use counting words. "I am going to the camper" where one cat and dog has been and has, I'm sure, told the other animals all about it. "I will be back in five days". I then use my fingers and say, "I will be gone Tuesday night for supper/bed", putting one finger up and holding the night feeding image in my head, "Wednesday night" a second finger, etcetera. I recap with showing fingers as I say "Tuesday, Wednesday, Thursday, Friday, Saturday and I'll be home Sunday before supper". They all know how it goes and I think already know the counting words and don't need all the mental images and details. Both dogs and cats will sit with ears in listening position, and when I'm done they go about their business. I feel information is power and when we all understand what's happening, it is easier to flow with events.

Lastly, I wish to share with you how I work with animals that aren't well and are hurting or sick or sad. It's tough on us, isn't it, when we don't know what to do for them? I certainly encourage you to follow your veterinarian's advice, and additionally, the below information may also assist you.

This is a little bit of my spiritual take on things regarding our beloved fur companions. They, just like us, have come into these bodies to have a life experience and have their own "contracts" shall we say, with their own souls. It is up to us to "back off" in our own distress around their pain or disabilities. We humans attach so much negative emotion to pain, but if we leave our "stuff" around what is happening out of the experience, things are much easier for our pet. For animals, pain is pain, and not pain is not pain. When we look at our friend, we may interpret a look as sorrow or suffering from pain or illness, when in fact it may be OUR suffering over THEIR pain they are reacting to.

When we make decisions around assisting a fur friend to leave their body and be free, we must PLEASE leave our guilt at the door. Of course we will be sad, sometimes absolutely lost and griefstricken after they leave. Yet, just like with our human family that leaves the body, we have done the best we could, loved them in the best way we knew, and "the body" isn't the end-all be-all. It is just a bunch of beautiful cells that are a blessing to experience and then leave behind for the greater experience of soul.

When I am present with my or another animal, I breathe calmly and open my awareness as much as I can. Sometimes I see red where they hurt. I may ask them questions out loud and listen deeply. Even if I don't "hear" an answer, I allow my hands to gently touch and explore calmly, because my Deepest Soul Self will know what to do, having heard the animal's communication. As I gently touch around the head in a caressing motion, for instance, I may find a knot or hot area and gently massage it. I'll ask the animal, "Is it sore here?" They always answer; with their eyes, with a lick of their tongue, with a deep sigh, or if I am particularly in-tune, I will just "get it" in a voice or a feeling. I continue the massage exploration, with an open easy heart and calm, gentle breath.

If you sit with your beloved fur companion, with gentle breath and open heart, you hands will certainly be guided. One doesn't need to "hear" or "see", but the felt sense in your hands is the ultimate wisdom. Trust it.

There are many animal massage therapists, energy workers, chiropractors and acupuncturists now available to us. There is also plenty of YouTube insight. My first exposure to working with animals was with the Tellington Touch or T-Touch. I do not know if she still lives in the Santa Fe area, but I was blessed to both read one of Linda

Tellington-Jones' first of many books and be in a small introductory workshop of hers in 1990 or 1991. She has successfully worked with many animals in therapeutic treatment or rehab all around the world, including animals with scales, claws, fins and hoofs! Learning a little of this work will not only help your animal but YOU, because this work can easily be applied to people, also. What could be better? Learning how to touch and breathe at the same time to our benefit and someone else's?

CHAPTER 23
Dream On

I know you have read or heard of the importance of dreams. Some of you may record them and interpret them. Some of you don't remember your dreams, and I also go through periods in my life when I do not remember my dreams. It makes me sad when I don't because I feel they are important in receiving information from my Deepest Soul Self, but I accept there are times in my life where dream recall must not be as important as other times.

However, if you can remember your dreams and do not already interpret them, I strongly suggest you start recording them and then interpret them. So herein lies the interesting question. How in the heck does one interpret dreams, and what school of dream interpretation does one follow?

In massage school, a wise friend of mine introduced me to Jungian dream interpretation which started my journey of investigating different forms of interpretation. I use my own interpretation process now, garnering others suggestions of what works well and creating what fits for me which led me into a reliable way of doing my own dream interpretation. I shall share this with you in case any of it is helpful.

These are the four types of dreams I have:

1. I have what I will call a "regular" dream where I experience a sometimes-pretty-weird story that seems to be a teaching story-line that I interpret when I awaken.

2. Or, in my dream, I am out visiting people, maybe even departed loved ones. Sometimes I am helping someone else, maybe someone I know or maybe a stranger. These dreams feel very real as if I saw that person, and in fact, I usually did!

3. I watch an action flick or another very compelling movie and I dream about it that night when I sleep.

4. I have either a precognition dream which is rare, or I am actually present during a tragedy, also rare.

The Number 1 dream and usually the Number 2 type dream I will take time to interpret as there is something either I am teaching myself or possibly someone else is teaching me. Even though I feel we are our own greatest teachers, sometimes there is "someone" in a dream I love and respect that may be actually visiting me to help me learn something I need to know. On the other hand, it may be the part of me that is similar to them that my psyche is bringing to the forefront. It can even be a person with which I have unresolved issues. Here is my condensed version of a regular dream interpretation:

My Dream: I drive to the grocery store in my car which keeps having power trouble. I press the accelerator but have only a sluggish response. I go into the store and go back to the produce department. Everyone is watching a weird thing going on. Lots of vegetables like swiss chard, kale and carrots are up in the air circling like a mini tornado out of gravity. We all stand around watching this phenomena. I eventually leave to continue my shopping. I wake up.

My Interpretation: Vehicles for me represent my body. Sometimes I have a low or flat front right tire which represents my right arm or maybe a bad rear left tire which refers to my left leg or foot. I know an old injury has been complaining to me and I haven't done what I know to do to help it, for instance.

So in this dream, the car's low power tells me my energy level isn't what it ought to be. Guess what! I also have been very scanty on proper eating which means I haven't been eating enough vegetables, especially leafy greens. I also promise myself to get to bed earlier for actual sleep, not excessive game playing time. This is simplistic but honestly, some times it is just a simple but important message.

If I dream of anyone else in number 1 or 2 type dreams, those people generally represent parts of myself. For instance, once in a dream a dear friend of mine represented the part of me that overworks. Another friend represented the part of me that is not giving myself enough good care and nurturance. My Mom part of me may be the self-nurturance part or may be my Divine Feminine energy.

Dream interpretation takes a little time to do, so set your clock earlier. Or write it down and come back to it after work. You have messages waiting!

Dream type Number 3 is what it is. Dream type Number 4, however, can be interesting. I woke up once not remembering my dream but I had an overwhelming feel of dread. Ick! A few hours later a large scale earthquake hit Indonesia. During my sleep I must have tapped in to a Universal energy or actually felt the premonition of the Earth shifting and knew what it meant. Another time, I dreamt of a helicopter full of soldiers crashing. A couple days later I read in the paper a helicopter going down killing several marines. I believe it happened in Afghanistan in the 2000's before the USA went into Iraq.

I had another dream that was not quite a dream that happened only once in my life. I was working from 9-12 and then 2-7 giving bodywork sessions. On my lunch break I would go home, have some lunch and then lay down and take a 20 minute, or so, nap. I love taking a nap after lunch, even now. Sometimes I fall completely asleep, but if I am getting good sleep at night, my rest time is a little different. I feel my etheric body come up a wee bit out of my body and I kind of daydream in a deeply resting state. I'll "wake up" before the alarm and be energized for the rest of my day!

This particular day I had an unusual experience and do not have perfect recall, although I could read through some journals to find all the specifics. I was taking my deep rest time this day, not completely asleep. I felt and saw myself going to a large city somewhere, travel up a set of narrow stairs in an apartment building and saw a man stabbing a woman. He opened the door and as he was leaving either she came out on her own or he partially dragged her out. He left. She fell and was on the stairs. I stopped and stayed with her as she died. I remember being completely calm and present. Her spirit came out of her body and she was confused, not sure what had happened. I conveyed to her she was okay now, she was safe, she was fine. I wanted to show her the beauty she could now have whenever she wanted, and we went out into space together. We went somewhere outside of our galaxy which we saw was so very beautiful. And then we saw the most fabulous nebula and the colors of that were exquisite and dazzling. I have a memory of seeing it before that time. Now I do not remember what happened next, but I feel certain her angels/guides/people were there to help her. I am certain I would not have left her alone.

I then "woke" up, although I was never fully asleep. I immediately was aware of a very large being in my room, that seemed "dark" colored, which was a little freaky to me after the experience I just had. But I also knew this being was one of "mine" and not to be feared. I got up and gratefully went back to work.

A few weeks later I saw my friend, who among many other skills and gifts, was the clearest Intuitive I knew. He saw the whole thing when I explained what happened and he said, yes, the being was one of my guides, but it was not dark at all but a light, colorful being and my human brain converted the color because I'd had little experience with my own guides at that point. I was still seeing through my fear.

This was about 25 years ago. This is my best guess and description of how it came to be that I assisted this woman in her transition. Everyone has guides/angels/ancestors who's jobs it is to help, guide and protect us. Some are with us always in this incarnation, and some are here for a period of time to assist us with new learning. Everyone who is "anybody" (all those guide peeps in the "guides club") know each other and I happened to be in the perfect place at the perfect time, meaning, my astral body was available and I was familiar with transitions and holding space for the same. I am certain we can have a conversation about time itself and Quantum Entanglement would explain what happened if indeed the math was put to the problem. For now, however, let's just say that basically, her people talked to my people and there I was!

So if you remember your dreams, or don't remember your dreams, the bottom line is we truly are here to help others. However, as our human selves evolve in learning how to be better lovers of our selves and each other, we must continue to learn true self-care and self-love. We are helping each other in this physical world in our own little or big way just as our souls are always helping us and each other.

CHAPTER 24
A Few Loose Ends

As I prepare to bring this share to a close, I realize there are a few important things I wish to relay that feel crucial for you to know and that don't necessarily fit into another chapter topic.

Mom and Dad divorced when I was in massage school. It was, as I am sure you can imagine, a very difficult time. They had been married for over 40 years and good or bad, a habit can be a tough thing to break. It was ultimately a relief for Mom and a tragedy for Dad. Staunch Catholic, remember? The unweaving of all those years to create separate lives was a painful task. They were not friends in their marriage to my Sister's and my thinking and observation, and they certainly weren't friends in their divorce.

Move forward seven years and Dad was diagnosed with cancer of the Parotid Gland which is the major salivary gland located in the left face/jaw area. He was scheduled for surgery a month after the diagnosis and was told it was very possible he would loose not only feeling in his face but also possibly movement of some facial muscles, even possibly affecting his ability to talk and eat.

Aunt Willa knew the diagnosis because she worked at Dad's MD's office and soon Mom also knew. These two faith-ladden, formidable women started treating Dad. Daily they arrived with a hot water bottle, a castor oil pack, prayers and other healing tools in their toolbox.

Willa was joy and laughter personified. She and Dad's relationship had always been very good as he had been like a big brother to her since she first met him at eight years of age. Mom and Dad's relationship began healing during these visits.

A month later, Aunt Willa and Dad traveled to Albuquerque for the surgery, and lo and behold, there was no surgery as there was no tumor! Prayers, energy work and good ol' Edgar Cayce castor oil packs won the day!

This breakthrough began a friendship between Mom and Dad I had not seen before. It built slowly and they were both in another loving relationship with someone else, but it was beautiful to behold. The years of love that had been partially buried within the dysfunction of their marriage arose to facilitate respect and caring for each other. Dad had his stroke several months before Mom passed and they were tender with each other during those several months. It was a precious sight and lesson: it is never to late to heal.

A powerfully painful event happened to Dad in World War II that I am positive caused much of his anger issues. He was 17 in 1942 when he joined the Army Air Corp and was assigned to a B-24 Liberator as the Radio Operator and waist-gunner. He was stationed in China, part of the CBI Theater (China/Burma/India), and flew what was considered the most dangerous route ever assigned to air transport. They would fly The Hump. This was a route over the Himalayan Mountains they flew from their base in China to India to fill their bomb bays with petrol. Heavily loaded they would return, hopefully staying intact enough to keep flying with no loss of life and make it back to the airfield. They could regularly expect enemy encounters. There were 659 aircraft lost and 1,659 personnel lost in these missions. They did this two days in a row and on the third day they would fly out over the (South) China Sea on bombing missions. They would then have one day off.

One Hump Day, the navigator was killed enroute and they were in trouble. Dad offered to triangulate radio waves which wasn't a common or normal navigation method in aviation at that point. He got them safely home. Because of this and unique equipment he would build on his days off, he was used in a secret mission.

One day, he was informed he would fly in a few hours with a pilot in a reconnaissance mission. He left as ordered in the night and they returned to base as the sky was lightening. He went to bed. When he awoke, he heard news of the atomic bomb being dropped by the Enola Gay on Hiroshima. His calculations were used to drop this first devastating weapon of the war. It was 50 years later before he could share that story.

There is another curious thing that occurred in World War II which personally affected me. Recall my death in the early part of the war. Great Britain declared war on Germany after Hitler invaded Poland in 1939, so my plane could feasibly have gone down from then on.

It wasn't until writing my story that I started investigating another incident. I had a deeply disturbing and profound dream in the early1980's which was possibly brought on by my British lifetime discovery. As I now ponder these events, I know I have recoiled from recalling or exploring anything about them. Even though I intentionally avoided researching around this dream and my "memories" throughout the years since the dream, I gleaned the dream pertained to the USS Indianapolis.

My experience: I awaken from a dream that feels like a memory. I can see in my minds eye hundreds of men in the ocean in various stages of death, dying and survival. Debris is all around and I know their ship has sunk from torpedo damage. During the daylight, shark fins can be seen everywhere it seems, as men are torn apart, piece by piece and then taken, many times in a frenzy of feeding. At night, when the waning moon is covered by clouds, only the moans and screams can be heard. I was there. I was not there.

This was the scene after the USS Indianapolis was torpedoed in the Pacific Ocean July 30, 1945, and shortly thereafter went down. The ship manifest was 1,195 men. It is estimated 300 went down with the ship in it's twelve minutes of death, 900 went into the water, and only 316 survived. Approximately 595 men died primarily from the results of shark attack. They were in the water for nearly four days before being accidentally discovered.

I have NEVER seen a film about this. There was a documentary in 2015, a feature film in 2016, PBS documentaries in 2017 and 2019 and a 2023 documentary. I have seen none of them. When I recently started to watch the 2023 documentary, the opening twelve seconds had me in a sob and I stopped watching.

The USS Indianapolis had a secret cargo of atomic bomb parts that were delivered to Tinian Island July 26. They then proceeded to Guam. On July 30th, halfway to the Leyte Gulf from Guam they were attacked by a Japanese submarine and sunk. They were not reported missing when they failed to arrive on July 31st. They were discovered on August 2.

The bomb parts were for Fat Boy which was dropped on Hiroshima August 6, 1945. August 5 was when my Dad was ordered to fly the recon mission to prepare for that August 6 drop.

Honestly, I had not put all these facts together in the same place because I had been avoiding doing so, and you my friends, have been a part of this discovery. If it had not been for you and my call to tell my story to you, I would not have discovered the fullness of the webs our souls weave and how fully connected we truly are.

I knew I needed to share my dream with you and my realization that I was actually there. My physical death had been about five years before, but as many times happens, I was with those men to assist however I could. Knowing what I know now, about how we truly are all angels on this Earth, I am positive there were many beings there helping the best they could in that crazy tragedy, just as I am positive there were even more assisting the mass of transitions that happened when that horrible bomb fell.

We are told from so many sources that there are many angels, guides, ancestors and other beings that assist when we transition. When there are huge tragedies here on Earth, there are huge "resource teams" that help those beloved souls transitions. I also understand there is celebration as the souls become aware of their true nature and that their body is a short-lived experience in the beauty of the fuller spirit.

We too, will someday "get it all" when we are done with these bodies. I for one, love being in this body and continue to enjoy every second I am blessed to be here! And true to New Mexico skies, I am stopping to go sit outside, kick my shoes off, lift my face to the sun, breathe and be grateful!

CHAPTER 25
It's a Wrap!

I was compelled to write this book for you and when I realized I needed to do this, I listened deeply and heard the words: "It is important." I thought I was writing the stories for you; for those of you that decided to pick this book to read because maybe YOUR guides or angels or ancestors put the book in your path. My hope is that it may help you become more confident in trusting your own instincts or intuition. My hope is that it may give you a few tools to start making sense of a life that doesn't make sense. My hope is that Earthing, the reality of healing that happens to your body, mind and spirit when you have your bare feet on the earth, your back pressed against a tree trunk, or when you sit with an appreciation of a wee bit of nature, these things becomes a loving commune of spirits. Your spirit and a plant or bird or spider, become a refuge and an answer. My hope is that you fall in love a little with your life again, that whimsey and wonder once again occur like it used to when you were tiny. My hope is that this book will cause you to remember and tell your story to someone. My hope is that you realize you are never alone and that you are so very, truly and deeply loved by many.

I thought I was writing this story for you. And I now know equally so, I was writing this story for me. For all those times where I don't feel like I am enough; that I didn't do enough, say enough, pray enough, work enough, here's to me! I have truly realized how important it is to take time to really see me. To acknowledge what I have been through in my life, how I persevered from places of brokenness, addiction, trauma, terror, loss and am still ok. I am loving myself a little better than I used to. I still get broken, deal with addictions sometimes, have old traumas I revisit for more release. And I am still ok. As my Mom used to say, "I am better and better, every day in every way."

I thank you for reading this book; I am filled with gratitude that you did. I hope you take a little time to appreciate some of the depths of despair and hard times you've had, and to remember to pat yourself on the back, ALOT, for how far you, too, have come! Be grateful for the small things and take some good care of you!

Marisalena
Roswell & Bent, New Mexico
April 1, 2024

About the Author

From motorcycles to massage, fiddle to finger cymbals, Marisalena's passions lead her down a colorful road of community and compassion. In addition to the above mentioned, she loves sharing the international Tai Chi for Health programs wherever she hangs her hat, and these days it is Roswell and the Ruidoso Mountains area of New Mexico.